Whitley Bay
Remembered
Part 2:
The Town Centre

by Charlie Steel

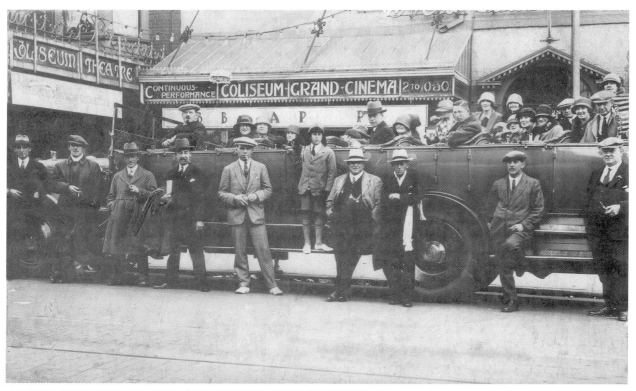

A charabanc outing outside the Coliseum Theatre and Grand Cinema. The occasion is unknown.

Previous page: Front Street, Whitley Bay – now a part of Whitley Road, that was once referred to as 'Rookery View'. This picture looks eastwards from St Paul's Church and shows the second Ship Inn to the centre of the picture, along with shops which still exist to this day. The stone wall and trees to the right, mark the corner of the grounds of Whitley Hall, subsequently occupied by the curved frontage of the building which for many years was better known as the Co-operative Store.

Copyright Charlie Steel 2016

First published in 2016 by

Summerhill Books
PO Box 1210
Newcastle-upon-Tyne
NE99 4AH

www.summerhillbooks.co.uk

email: summerhillbooks@yahoo.co.uk

ISBN: 978-1-911385-01-1

CONTENTS

THE LOCAL WEEKLY NEWSPAPER. And VISITORS' GAZETTE. For WHITLEY, CULLERCOATS, TYNEMOUTH AND DISTRICT.

ACKNOWLEDGEMENTS & CONTRIBUTORS

It is only with the assistance of others that a publication of this nature can be successfully produced. I am therefore particularly grateful to the undermentioned individuals and organisations for their valued contributions:

ITEM	CONTRIBUTOR
Coliseum Cinema	Anne Pexton, Wirral, Merseyside
Nicholsons Butchers, Park View	Doug & Kathryn Nicholson, Whitley Bay
Finlay & Sons, Park View	Michael Finlay, Whitley Bay
Featonby's, Park View	Gill Featonby, Whitley Bay
McCaughey, Whitley Road	Christopher Carr (Splinters Hairdressing), Whitley Bay
Regent Street	Peter Hasselby, Whitley Bay
Whitley Bay in the '70s	Chris Wilson, Kirkharle, Northumberland

Special thanks also go to Andrew Clark (Summerhill Books), Whitley Bay Masonic Hall Co. Ltd, Staff of North Shields Local Studies Centre, Ordnance Survey Mapping, Northumbria Police and North Tyneside Council for the relevant contributions.

SOURCES OF REFERENCE:

Cinemas of North Tyneside   Frank Manders
Ward's Directories 1850-1940   R. Ward & Sons
Kelly's Directories 1894-1938
Blair's Directories 1968
Various vintage Whitley Bay Guidebooks
'Rockcliffe Remembers' Website   Mick Sharp & Black Dog Design

PREFACE

Whitley Bay Remembered – Part 1 was published in October 2015 and covered the Coastal strip and its associated history between St Mary's Island and the Cullercoats boundary. This is *Part Two*, which complements that edition and concentrates on the town centre and former village of Whitley, by looking at its development through the streets, buildings shops and trades which have existed here over the years and have been fundamental in its evolution.

Today, like many other town centres throughout the country, Whitley Bay has suffered with shop closures because of a massive drop in retail trade which is probably attributable to a number of factors.

Prior to the 1980s, most retail shopping was done in town and city centres, however the concept of retail parks and out of town supermarkets and shopping centres sprang up as a result of the increase in car ownership and these now account for a substantial loss of local trade. This in turn is exacerbated by internet shopping which also plays a significant role in taking away valuable trade from our local economy.

Sadly, only a small handful of established enterprises remain, but in the 'Good old Days', Whitley Bay flourished with almost every kind of business and shop imaginable: Butchers, Bakers, Cobblers, Tailors, Jewellers, Cafes and Drapers – the list is practically endless. These businesses were once a vital part of the community and rendered the town almost self-sufficient.

By today's standards, it is very difficult to perceive the bygone array of different businesses, all of which operated so close together. The shops and frontages were neat and tidy, window displays were large and varied and the signage above the shops was artistic and self-explanatory. Windows and steps were cleaned daily, door brasses were polished and a lot of pride and effort was taken to attract, welcome and maintain customers.

This book reflects on those years where happy memories will be recalled and good times are remembered.

Charlie Steel
May 2016

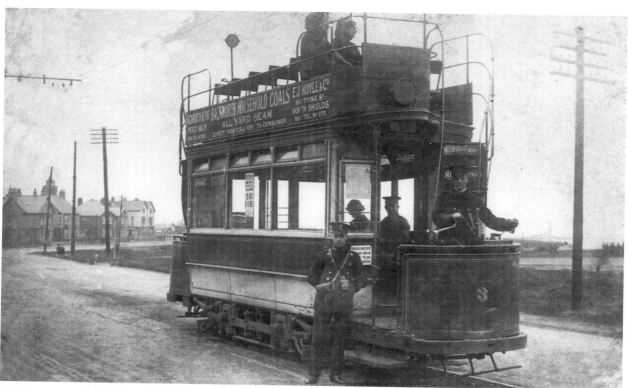

A Tynemouth & District Electric Traction Co. Tramcar at the new Bandstand Terminus on Whitley Links, c.1904.

A SHORT HISTORICAL OVERVIEW

The origins of Whitley can be traced back to its establishment in 1116 when it was little more than a tiny hamlet owned by the Prior of Tynemouth. The name of the village can also be attributed to the de Whitley family, local landowners who held a manor house in the area up to 1538.

John Speede's map of 1610 shows the spelling as 'Whitlathe', the area of which extended from what is now the corner of the present Station Road to the corner of Marden Road.

By 1674, following the dissolution of the monasteries, the Priory lands and estate were enclosed and divided up, except for Whitley Links which to this day remains as open land.

In 1760, Whitley Hall was built by Henry Hudson, a local landowner, and occupied the area of land now enclosed by Marden Road, Whitley Road (Front Street), Victoria Terrace, and the present railway line (see page 12).

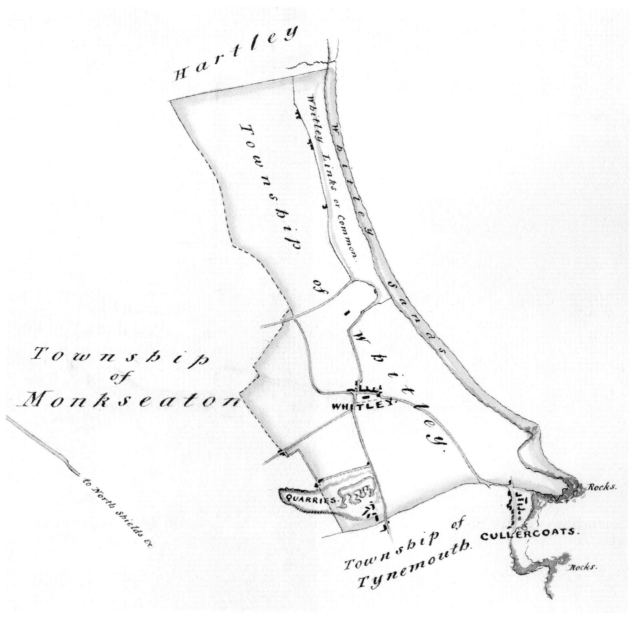

Following a survey in 1757 by J. Thompson, this map indicates the extent of Whitley Township and shows a small number of buildings which built up to form the present town centre. The roads shown, follow the same pattern today and highlight what are now The Links, Marine Avenue, Park Avenue, Park View, Whitley Road, Hillheads Road and Marden Road.

St Paul's Church was built in 1864, and the Prudhoe Convalescent Homes in 1866 followed by the Northumberland Village Homes which were opened in 1880.

By the 1870s, land was being built up in small sections between Front Street and Rockcliffe, with many shops, large houses and hotels being constructed on the seafront.

In 1882 the North Eastern Railway opened its new coastal line, and this led to the rapid growth of Whitley as both a seaside resort and a commuter town.

At one time known simply as 'Whitley' or 'Whitley-by-the-Sea', it is widely held that Whitley Bay derived its present name from local indignation at the confusion between the place names Whitley and Whitby during the late 1800s.

Since its early beginnings, Whitley Bay has transformed from a tiny hamlet, to a small village, and eventually to the residential and commercial town that exists today.

A more comprehensive overview of Whitley Bay is outlined in *Whitley Bay Remembered – Part 1.*

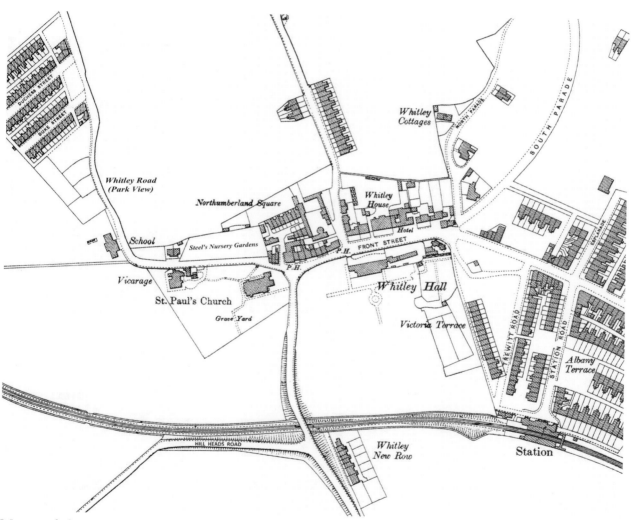

Many of the places, streets and buildings shown on this 1895 map of Whitley Village are featured in this book, and when used in conjunction with the relevant articles, should prove to be a useful guide and reference source.

HOUSING AND STREET DEVELOPMENT

The development of Whitley Bay as a residential area began in the mid 1800s. By the 1870s, land was being built up in small sections between Front Street and Rockcliff, with many shops, and houses being constructed in the district. Two prominent builders in the area at this time were Richard Heckels Nesbitt and Alfred Styan, who were responsible for laying out many of the streets and much of the housing towards the south side of Whitley.

Victoria Terrace c.1910.

Between 1860 and 1898, North Parade, South Parade, The Esplanade and Station Road had been laid out, and by 1918, a number of residential streets around the town centre had also been built. There was at this time, a mix of both pride and regret at the speed of the town's growth. Over the years that followed, the boundary of the town had already extended south towards Cullercoats, and thereafter, soon extended towards Brier Dene in the north, and Monkseaton Village in the west.

During the residential development of Whitley, the significant building periods for some of the older streets in the district are grouped into the following dates:

Pre-1860
Whitley Road (Front Street)

1860-1898

Albany Gardens	East Parade	Percy Road
Algernon Place	Edwards Road	South Parade
Alma Place	Egremont Place	Station Road
Countess Avenue	Esplanade	Trewitt Road
Delaval Road	Grafton Road	Victoria Avenue
Duke Street	Marine Avenue	
Duchess Street	North Parade	

1898-1918

Albert Terrace	Clarence Crescent	Helena Avenue
Alexandra Terrace	Cliftonville Gardens	Holly Avenue
Alma Place	Clifton Terrace	Holywell Avenue
Alnwick Avenue	Clovelly Gardens	Ilfracombe
Ashfield Grove	Collingwood Terrace	Gardens
Balmoral Gardens	Coquet Avenue	Jesmond Terrace
Beach Avenue	Cromer Gardens	Kew Gardens
Beech Grove	Eastbourne Gardens	Kings Drive
Bideford Gardens	Eskdale Terrace	Kings Road
Bournemouth Gardens	Esplanade Avenue	Laburnum Avenue
Briar Avenue	Esplanade Place	Linden Terrace
Brighton Grove	Evesham Avenue	Lish Avenue
Brook Street	Gladstone Avenue	Mafeking Street
Burnfoot Terrace	Gladstone Terrace	(Fern Avenue)
Charles Avenue	Gordon Square	Marden Crescent
Cheviot View	Grosvenor Drive	Margaret Road
Claremont Gardens	Hawthorn Gardens	Marine Gardens

Mason Avenue
Naters Street
Norham Road
Ocean View
Osborne Gardens
Oxford Street
Park Avenue
Park Parade
Park Road
Percy Avenue
Percy Road

Queens Drive
Queens Road
Rockcliffe Avenue
Rockcliffe Gardens
Rockcliffe Street
Roxburgh Terrace
Stanley Crescent
Swinbourne Gardens
Styan Avenue
The Avenue
The Crescent

Tynedale Avenue
Ventnor Gardens
Victoria Terrace
Warkworth Avenue
Waterford Crescent
Windsor Avenue
Windsor Crescent
Windsor Gardens
Windsor Terrace
York Road

1918-1938

Amble Avenue
Belsay Avenue
Belvedere Avenue
Chestnut Avenue
Chollerford Avenue
Claremont Road
Davison Avenue
Dilston Avenue
Dowling Avenue
Etal Avenue
Felton Avenue
Glendale Avenue

Grasmere Crescent
Haig Avenue
Hillheads Road
Hobart Terrace
Holystone Avenue
Hotspur Avenue
Kingsley Avenue
Links Avenue
Lovaine Avenue
Maderia Avenue
Marden Road South
Monkseaton Drive

Percy Gardens
Plessey Crescent
Priory Avenue
Richmond Terrace
Roker Avenue
St Marys Avenue
St. Pauls Gardens
Shaftesbury Avenue
Studley Gardens
Sycamore Avenue

Some of the earliest houses in Whitley Bay date back to the Victorian and Edwardian eras, and were designed as large terraced residences, usually incorporating a garden, bounded by a wall or decorative iron railings and fronted by a pedestrian footpath or walkway. It was usual for ornate iron posts to be placed at each end of the street, which were intended to limit or restrict the movement of non-pedestrian traffic. As a result, the houses were typically accommodated with a back yard and serviced by a rear lane. A majority of these picturesque streets were laid out towards the south of the main town centre between Whitley Road and its boundary with the present railway line, although other similar streets are also evident throughout the town.

Cambridge Avenue c.1912.

Pedestrianised Streets

Albany Gardens
Albert Terrace
Alexandra Terrace
Alnwick Avenue
Cambridge Avenue
Charles Avenue
Clarence Crescent
Countess Avenue
Crescent Vale

Devonshire Terrace
Elmwood Grove
Esplanade Avenue
Gladstone Terrace
Gordon Terrace
Helena Avenue
Linden Terrace
Lish Avenue
Mason Avenue

Percy Avenue
Rockcliffe Avenue
Styan Avenue
The Crescent
Trewitt Road
Victoria Avenue
Warkworth Avenue

WHITLEY BAY POPULATIONS

A census is a complete population count for a given area or place taken on a specific date. The 1841 census is considered to be the first modern UK version, however returns were also submitted before that time, and the earliest count for Whitley Village appears to have taken place in 1801.

The table below shows the population of Whitley Village from 1801 and how it has gradually increased over the years. The figures do not include Monkseaton Village.

1801	251	
1811	375	
1821	554	
1831	632	
1841	749	
1851	431	(This drop was due to the laying-in of Whitley Colliery)
1861	419	
1871	731	
1881	1,350	
1891	2,444	(Population almost doubled in 10 years due to new housing)
1901	7,705	
1911	14,410	
1921	22,250	
1931	24,203	
1935	27,130	
1946	31,000	
1951	32,520	

WHITLEY BAY ACREAGES

These figures indicate the area of open space, parkland and recreational areas in both Whitley and Monkseaton in 1954:

Whitley Links	74.50 acres
Hillheads Recreation Grounds	12.00 acres
Churchill Playing Fields	10.00 acres
Langley Playing Fields	9.50 acres
Souter Park	6.64 acres
Whitley Park	3.74 acres
Crawford Park	1.77 acres
Victoria Park	1.24 acres
Marmion Terrace Playground	1.05 acres
Brook Street Gardens	0.74 acres
Rockcliffe Park	0.54 acres

Additionally – there were 38.21 acres of allotment land throughout the Borough.

An aerial view of Whitley Bay in 1927.

Focusing on St Paul's Church and its grounds to the centre of the picture, Marden Road in the foreground runs diagonally towards the lower right corner of the image.

Much of the town centre is clearly evident with the Ship Corner, Belvedere Buildings, Coliseum Cinema and the Victoria Hotel visible towards the right edge, along with part of Laburnum Avenue. Oxford Street Garage and North Parade can be seen to the extreme upper right corner and to the lower foreground, Whitley Bay Motor Company is prominent on Marden Road.

Steel's Market Gardens can be seen to the left of, and opposite St Paul's Churchyard. The Fat Ox Pub is the building beyond the spire of the church, and the row of terraced houses behind was part of the area formerly referred to as Northumberland Square. (Steel's market gardens also extended behind these houses and occupied part of the land known as Hickey's Dairy Farm.)

The large building at the edge of these gardens is the General Post Office and the remaining rows of houses to the upper section are Park Avenue, Cambridge Avenue and Oxford Street.

WHITLEY HALL

Records indicate that Whitley Hall was built between 1757 and 1769 by the family of Henry Hudson, a local landowner, however the actual building date can be pinpointed to 1760. As a manor-house, it was encircled by a stone boundary wall and up to the end of the 1800s, the centre of Whitley Village was almost entirely occupied by its spacious grounds.

In 1817, the hall was sold to the Duke of Northumberland, and was a typical old country residence where its tenants lived well with their coachmen, gardeners, and large staff of servants. The main entrance to the hall was opposite St Paul's Church on what is now Marden Road, where the curved frontage of the former Co-operative store was situated. The Hall itself faced south towards the present railway line. The grounds were thickly wooded and home to a conclave of thousands of rooks which loaned their name to a part of Whitley Road which was once known as 'Rookery View'.

The actual hall was demolished in 1899, and stood on the exact site of what was later to become the Police Station in Laburnum Avenue. The grounds were levelled to make way for the development of residential streets and houses which now comprise: Victoria Terrace, Laburnum Avenue, Fern Avenue, Jesmond Terrace, Clifton Terrace, The Crescent and Crescent Vale as well as the southern side of Whitley Road between Marden Road and Victoria Terrace.

Interestingly, the street which connects Clifton Terrace and Laburnum Avenue was originally called Mafeking Street and was probably dedicated as such following the relief of Mafeking during the Boer War. For some reason, this street name was changed to Fern Avenue sometime after 1940, however the reason for this is unclear.

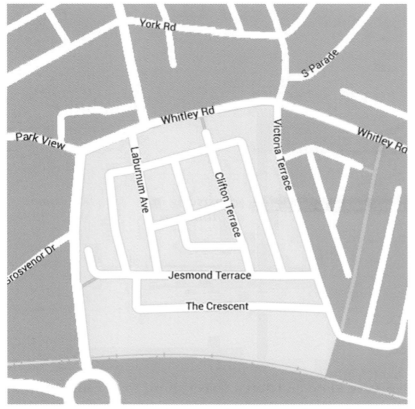

A current street plan showing the extent of Whitley Hall grounds.

FRONT STREET (WHITLEY ROAD)

The centre of Whitley Village has always been defined as the area between St Paul's Church to the site of the old smithy (latterly Woolworths corner). Although rarely referred to as such these days, Front Street is the section of road that connects these points and is now broadly incorporated within Whitley Road. The buildings situated between the Fat Ox public House and the former Ship Inn are the oldest known in Whitley and were generally referred to as 'Rookery View' as they originally faced the

grounds of Whitley Hall which stood opposite on the site of what later became the Co-op store built in 1902.

The old smithy (pictured right), which stood proud of the road close to the corner of Front Street and Oxford Street had been owned and run since the early 1850s by a Thomas Charlton who resided in the cottage next door. Known as Charlton's Smithy, it was demolished in 1910 and replaced in 1924 by a branch of F.W. Woolworth.

Covered in ivy, the picture (below) shows Belvedere House, built around 1800 by a Henry Coward on the site of an older house dating to the late 1600s when it was the home of a John Dove, an extensive local landowner. In 1804, the premises came under the ownership of a Mr Peregrine Henzell, an entrepreneur in the Tyneside glass industry.

This building stood on the corner of Front Street and Park Avenue until it was replaced in 1926 by the present Belvedere buildings. (This view looks north east from the corner of Laburnum Avenue.)

In March 1806, it was referred to in the Newcastle Courant as *'A new capital dwelling house consisting of a Drawing Room, Dining Room, 8 Lodging Rooms, 2 Kitchens, a large Garden, Vinery and Peach House, a double Coach House, 2 Stables and a Coach House.'*

Thereafter, the building changed hands a number of times before coming into the possession of R.A. Jackson, a well-known local estate agent, after which the Belvedere Property Co. Ltd was established.

Some of the well established businesses that formed part of the Belvedere Buildings, particularly during the 1950s, were Sampson's fruiterers occupying the corner site, followed by the 'Belvedere Baccy Box', a tiny tobacconists next door which was adjoined by the famous Belvedere Pork Shop and Toft's Sweet shop. An arcade then separated the buildings from the Coliseum Cinema and the Victoria public house.

REGENT STREET (Whitley Road)

The south side of Front Street between Laburnum Avenue and Victoria Terrace was sub-named Regent Street. The image above dates to c.1910 when the road in front of the shops was adorned with trees. The Central Hall buildings at the top of South Parade are visible in the distance. In the foreground, Park Avenue runs off to the left and Laburnum Avenue to the right.

A stone plaque (shown left), marks the existence of Regent Street, and is still evident to this day. It is situated between the upper dormer windows of the first two shops on the street.

COLISEUM THEATRE AND CINEMA

Located on Front Street (Whitley Road) in the centre of Whitley Bay, the Coliseum Theatre was built in neo-classical style and opened in May 1910 to provide live entertainment. Prior to which, a doctor's house and fruiterers stood on the site. Building work commenced in 1909 by a Mr William Smelt, and on Whit Saturday 1910, the New Coliseum Theatre was opened by the Mayor of Tynemouth with a number of local councillors making up the stage party for this grand occasion. Mrs Bella Matheson, a Cullercoats fishwife who was widely known throughout the Whitley and Tynemouth district as 'Bella the Lifeboat Lady', was present on the Coliseum's first night, and thereafter attending almost every week for the next 40 years. Plush carpets were fitted throughout the building and the fittings, curtains and décor were admired by many. An organ was installed at a cost of £4,000 and to see a show in 1910, cost 4d, with Saturday matinees for children costing 2d.

In 1914, at the outbreak of the First World War, the cinema was requisitioned by the military authorities for use as a billet. When the military moved out, the theatre required extensive refurbishment and modernisation work, and therefore in 1919 the premises were taken over by a Mr William Baker who was a Northern Cinema pioneer and became a director of the New Coliseum Company. A total of £40,000 was spent on alterations and the theatre was converted to a picture hall, re-opening for business in 1920 under the name of 'The New Coliseum Cinema' where many silent films were shown over the years.

In December 1929, following 18 months of negotiations, the Coliseum was purchased by the A.B.C. (Associated British Cinema) group from the Baker family. Further refurbishment work was undertaken which included removal of the organ which was sold, however the stage area remained and the seating capacity was increased to accommodate 1,299 persons. New wiring was fitted to update the premises which allowed the screening of some of the first 'Talkies'.

The first 'Talkie' film to be shown at the cinema was screened on 20th January 1930 entitled 'Bulldog Drummond'.

The Coliseum cinema c.1930 during refurbishment work.

Thereafter, the cinema remained in constant use up to October 1970 when it was taken over by a local businessman; Mr Harry Swaddle. The doors finally closed on 1st May 1971 when the last film, 'Dirty Dingus Magee' was screened before its conversion to a Bingo Club.

Plans were passed in 2004 to allow demolition of the former auditorium, as a result of which offices and a new library were later constructed to the rear of the site. The front of the building and the main façade were retained and remained as retail shops.

The New Coliseum Cinema in 1982 after its conversion to a bingo hall and shops.

WHITLEY COUNCIL OFFICES

In 1873, the Reverend R.F. Wheeler of St Paul's Church was instrumental in forming the first Local Board, which consisted of just twelve members. This board was a forerunner of the council and looked after the local affairs of both Whitley and Monkseaton Parishes.

On 18th November 1894, the district of the Local Board was superseded by the first Urban District Council which also consisted of twelve members. As a result, a new council building (below) was constructed on a site situated directly next to the Victoria Hotel on Whitley Front Street and comprised a Council Chamber, Committee Rooms and various offices. The opening date was 1st June 1901 but by 1955 it became inadequate for purpose when Councillors and members of the public complained about the difficulty of talking privately with officials as the building became overcrowded. As a result, the council moved into 'temporary' offices next to the Priory Theatre at the foot of Park Avenue. In the meantime, some conversion work was carried out to the ground floor to accommodate two retail shops before the building was eventually demolished after a 54 year lifespan, which also made way for the rebuilding of the nearby Woolworths Store. A side lane was retained to provide access to the Fire Station situated to the rear of the building.

By 1908, four wards had been established in Whitley, comprising Rockcliff, Marden, St Mary's and Monkseaton. Over the years, further ward boundaries came into being and on 1st April 1935, parts of the old Urban Districts of Seaton Delaval and Earsdon were added which included the two villages of Old Hartley and Seaton Sluice. The area was then divided into eight wards each returning three councillors.

In 1943, the council made application to the Northumberland County Council for consent to change the name and so on 1st January 1944 the Whitley and Monkseaton Urban District became the Whitley Bay Urban District. On 5th March 1954 the town was granted its Royal Charter of Incorporation as the Borough of Whitley Bay. The charter was presented by HRH the Princess Royal at a ceremony in the town on 14th April 1954. In 1974, the Local Government Act abolished the borough, with Hartley in the north going to Blyth Valley district in Northumberland, and the main part including Whitley and Monkseaton forming part of the Metropolitan Borough of North Tyneside in the newly-named 'Tyne and Wear' area.

WHITLEY ROAD

Prior to the 1860s, Whitley Road was little more than a country lane and it was during this decade that the area of land to the south east of Whitley Village began to undergo both housing and commercial development.

Whitley Road is the longest street in the town and originally ran from the Cullercoats boundary with John Street, northwards through the town centre eventually ending at the junction with Marine Avenue. In 1926, part of the road was renamed as Park View and, nowadays, Whitley Road effectively ends at St Paul's Church.

By the 1890s, construction work had begun on many of the larger buildings on the section of Whitley Road between its junctions with Oxford Street and the Esplanade to become the main shopping area. Terracotta and stone plaques are evident on the upper storeys of various buildings on both sides of the road indicating the respective years of construction.

A number of smaller sub-named streets were incorporated into Whitley Road. At the southern end was St Mary's Terrace and Carlton Terrace, then Wilfred Terrace, Arcadia and Catherine Terrace. Whitley Road then continues as far as Victoria Terrace where it encompasses Front Street to the east side and Regent Terrace to the west side. These names have long since disappeared from use.

Whitley Town Centre c.1952.

CATHERINE TERRACE

Situated on the southwest corner of Whitley Road and Algernon Terrace, Catherine Terrace consists of just 8 houses which were originally numbered from 1 to 8. The houses have since been incorporated to form part of the main street, as a result of which they were later re-numbered as Nos. 145 to 159 Whitley Road. The houses are amongst the oldest in Whitley and were built in 1867 by a Mr John Pratt.

A date-stone (above) which incorporates the street name is evident by a plaque situated between the first floor windows in mid-terrace.

It is claimed that the street was named after the wife of one of the first occupants, Catherine Hunter.

A general view of Whitley Road c.1925, looking south towards Cullercoats. The houses forming Catherine Terrace are situated to the right of the image, Arcadia shops are towards the centre and Trinity Methodist Church is situated behind the wall (off-camera) to the left.

WHITLEY ROAD
BUILDINGS AND SHOPS

ASSEMBLY BUILDINGS

The Assembly Rooms situated at 220 Whitley Road, together with the adjoining shops were built for a Mr John Addison Smith in 1895, and a decorative square terracotta plaque bearing the date and his initials is still evident between the first floor windows. It is probable that there were no other buildings on Whitley Road at this time and this was one of the first to be constructed on this section of the street.

Smith leased the Assembly Rooms to the Whitley Sports Club, which opened on 8th May 1914 with a membership of over 200 men who had subscribed to use the lounge, reading, billiard and games rooms.

Shops were situated to the ground floor of the premises, to each side of the arched entrance doorway. The shop to the right was that of Frederick Mason's small bakery chain which was originally based in North Shields. Mr Mason died in 1905 and the business then moved to the corner of Victoria Terrace. The shop to the left was that of Walter Kerr, a fancy stationer who moved here from Newcastle in 1890 (see page 26).

In 1901, part of the first floor was occupied by a Mr Giovanni Povesi who was the proprietor of the Assembly Dining Rooms. Mr Povesi also ran a café on Sydenham Terrace which is referred to in *Whitley Bay Remembered – Part 1*.

A front view of the Assembly Rooms showing the significant arched entrance, and shops to the ground floor.

An eloquent and colourful description of Mr Povesi's business taken from a 1901 guidebook states: *'It is probably not too much to say that the rapid rise of many of our seaside resorts is due directly to the efforts of the restauranteur and hotel proprietor. To these intelligent and enterprising persons, in any case, no small measure of the comfort which now characterises them, as compared with the general discomfort of former times, may be justly attributed; the advance in the line of catering and general provision for the wants of the travelling and visiting public having been remarkably great in the last few years.*

'The Assembly Dining Rooms, Whitley, of which Mr Giovanni Povesi is the proprietor, exemplifies this improvement in a marked degree. The premises are not more than a minute from the station, and easily accessible. The accommodation includes spacious and well-furnished dining rooms, large ballroom, private dining-rooms, ladies' rooms, reading rooms, smoke rooms etc, and the cuisine is first-class in every respect. Hot dinners are served from 12 to 2 (separate tables), and teas, suppers, chops, steaks, fish

etc are furnished at the shortest notice. The rooms are open on Sundays from May to October, and special accommodations are provided for cyclists. The charges in all cases are moderate and the service excellent. We may add that Mr Povesi was formerly chef at the Hotel Des-iles-Britanniques, San Remo, Riviera.'

Above: The Assembly Building looking south.

Below: The Assembly Building looking north.

WHITLEY ROAD SHOPS

As Whitley Bay grew from what was once a village into a town, it soon became a place where the demand for goods, products and services was high, as a result of which, numerous retail trades and businesses developed and were quickly established. Whitley Road was the main thoroughfare through the middle of the town, so inevitably it became the main focal shopping centre where dozens of different outlets soon began to dominate the street. Businesses flourished with every kind of shop imaginable, Butchers, Bakers, Cobblers, Tailors, Jewellers, Cafe's and Drapers – the list is practically endless which meant that the town was at one time virtually self-sufficient.

By today's standards, it is very difficult to perceive the array of different businesses, all of which operated so close together. The shops and frontages were neat and tidy, window displays were large and varied and the signage above the shops was artistic and self-explanatory. Windows and steps were cleaned daily, door brasses were polished and a lot of pride was taken to attract customers.

The following pages list only a mere fraction of those early businesses that were once evident on this street. It is however particularly important to note that between 1936-38, many of the premises on Whitley Road were re-numbered, but followed no consistent pattern, as a result of which, not all properties can be determined or easily synchronised with those bearing the same street number today. This is more significant with the odd-numbered properties.

ARCADIA

Arcadia was the name given to the small row of shops built by Mr Alfred Styan on the north side of Whitley Road, which are now numbered 130 to 154. A stone plaque set into the upper wall of the building indicating, 'Arcadia 1899' is still evident.

The name 'Arcadia' was derived from a wrought iron and glass canopy which was once attached to the frontages of these buildings and extended over the adjoining footpath to form a stylish ornate façade. This style of Victorian architecture typified many similar shops of the period in other seaside resorts throughout the country.

When Arcadia opened, it would appear that the first building at No. 154 became a chemists shop which, up to 1924 was run by a Mr George Whitehead. Although the business changed hands several times since, it continued trading as a chemist or pharmacy retaining this status, and in 2016 was recorded as a branch of 'Boots' chemists.

Next door to this shop, Mr William Arthur Laws ran a cycle dealers which he advertised as the oldest and largest cycle dealers in the district. He later left here to extend his business and open larger premises known as the Exchange Buildings at the top of South Parade (see page 55). The Arcadia shop was later taken over by a Jessie Hamilton to become a tobacconist, and later a drapers shop by a Mr Charles Krawitz.

There appears to be no accurate record of when the ironwork and glass façade was removed from the buildings.

McCAUGHEY
Baker & Confectioner, 62 Whitley Road. Proprietor James McCaughey.
In 2016 these premises were trading as Splinters Hairdressing Salon.

James McCaughey's bakery shop at 62 Whitley Road, dates to 1928 when it first appeared in local trades directories. This image of the shop below also dates to around 1928, where it may be reasonably assumed that the man standing in the centre is Mr McCaughey, however the remaining group of people remain unidentified.

It seems that by 1940, the business had been taken over by Northern Traders Ltd where it continued as a confectionery shop. Over the years, the premises changed hands a number of times and eventually became a branch of Crawfords Bakers.

In 1981 the shop was taken over by Mr Alan Moat and Mr Christopher Carr, to become 'Splinters' Hair Salon. Interestingly, it transpired that a large concrete lintel situated at the back of the salon supported an opening into the house next door (No. 60) which once housed ovens for baking the bread.

In 1981 the shop front was exactly the same as it had been in the 1920s, but was in a very poor condition. Although every effort was made to retain the old facade, restoration costs proved too great and a reluctant decision was made to change to the modern shop front that can be seen today.

J.W. SHAW

Wine & Spirit Dealer, 112 & 162 Whitley Road.
Proprietor Mr John W. Shaw.

John Shaw ran his Wine & Spirit Business from 112 Whitley Road, later opening a smaller shop at 162 Whitley Road, as depicted on the image right. This shop was situated on the corner of Whitley Road and Percy Road and although the business no longer exists, these small premises still survive and in 2016 were trading as a tattoo parlour.

Mr W.J. BULLOCK

Confectioner and Fancy Bread Baker,
129 Whitley Road.
Proprietor Mr William James Bullock.
Re-numbered as 181 Whitley Road, trading as the Shikara Indian Restaurant in 2016.

William James Bullock was a well-known baker and confectioner who had premises in Whitley Bay for many years. In 1901, his premises were situated at No. 129 Whitley Road and from a guidebook of that year his business was colourfully outlined as follows: *'The importance of pure and well baked bread cannot be over-estimated in the welfare of any community. Whitley however is in no danger of failure in this respect, the above establishment, of which Mr W.J. Bullock is the proprietor, having a thoroughly deserved reputation for supplying light and well baked bread composed of the best cereal ingredients and made on the best hygienic principles. His connection is especially large throughout the district in this department; the excellence of his production in the bread line being widely recognised. The shop is situated in the best part of the town, and is a model of its class for cleanliness and neat arrangement. All kinds of wholesome and carefully made confectionery are kept on hand; cakes, jellies, ices, cordials, fancy breads and other appetising articles being always obtainable. A supply of fresh cakes may be depended on at all times. Among specialities of the business, Hovis bread may be mentioned, with Fry's and Cadbury's chocolates and other staples of the kind. The show windows are always neatly arranged, and a tempting stock of eatables displayed. Customers are always assured of prompt attention and moderate prices are the invariable rule.'*

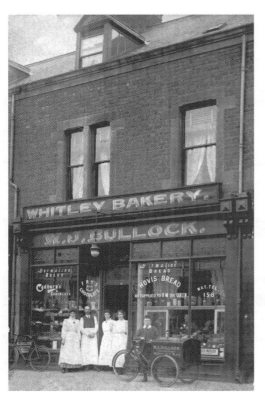

S. MORTIMER

Draper, 131 Whitley Road.
Proprietor Sam Mortimer.
Re-numbered as 183 Whitley Road,
trading as Antonio's Italian Restaurant
in 2016.

W. J. SPARKES

Drapers, 153 Whitley Road.
Proprietor W.J. Sparkes.
Re-numbered as 201 Whitley Road,
trading as Tiger Bills Restaurant in 2016.

Formerly Young and Aiston's drapery store, Sparke's drapery store stood on the corner of Whitley Road and Station Road. The upper floor consisted of meeting rooms which later became the Coast Club. (Refer to Station Road on page 40.)

ALEX Y. STEEL

Jeweller, Goldsmith & Watchmaker,
157 Whitley Road.
Proprietor Mr Alexander Y. Steel.
Re-numbered as 205 Whitley Road,
trading as Automoney in 2016.

Alexander Steel ran a jewellery business on Whitley Road, from the early 1900s. During the 1930s the business expanded to include an opticians. The shop later became better known as Steel & Varley (Opticians) and in later years moved to different premises just a couple of doors away where the business mostly concentrated on eyecare.

EVANS & Co.

Milliners and Drapers, 171 & 173 Whitley Road.
Re-numbered as 219 & 221 Whitley Road, trading as the
Singer Sewing Shop and Runamokka in 2016.

Situated at No. 171 Whitley Road, Evans millinery shop had a corner frontage that
extended into Trewitt Road where it was adorned by a wrought iron and glass canopy.

The drapery shop which was also part of the business was situated at No. 173 Whitley Road (the adjoining corner of Trewitt Road).

An interesting stone plaque (below) situated on the corner gable of this building indicates 'Jubilee Buildings 1897', presumably to represent the Diamond Jubilee of Queen Victoria during that year.

Another interesting image (below) shows a crowded charabanc outside Evans Store, however the occasion is unknown.

G.T. FORBES

Jeweller, Watchmaker and Optician,
187 Whitley Road.
Proprietor Mr George T. Forbes.
Original premises were demolished along
with neighbouring shops to be rebuilt as
225-233 Whitley Road, trading as
SS Healthfoods in 2016.

WALTER KERR

Artistic Household Goods and Fancy
Stationer, Assembly Buildings,
Whitley Road.
Re-numbered as 222 Whitley Road,
trading as Kebab King in 2016.

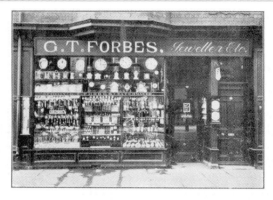

If you require a useful Present or
Dainty Souvenir at a moderate price,
INSPECT MY STOCK OF
GOLD, SILVER, AND ART JEWELLERY.
SILVER-MOUNTED ARTICLES for the Toilet Table.
NOVELTIES IN ELECTRO-PLATE, FANCY GOODS,
LEATHER BAGS AND PURSES, CUTLERY, etc.

G. T. FORBES,

Watchmaker, Optician, &c.,
187, WHITLEY ROAD, Whitley Bay.
Agent for the ONOTO PEN.

Walter Kerr's shop was situated on the ground floor of the Assembly Buildings on Whitley Road. An extract from a 1901 guidebook describes the business as follows: '*Without question, the largest and most complete establishment for the sale of stationery and its adjuncts in Whitley and the district is that carried on by Mr Walter Kerr at the address given above. The position, we need not say, is excellent and the shop is a model of good arrangement and taste. A very attractive show is made both in the windows and in stock in the way of fancy stationery of all kinds, photographs and frames, purses, leather goods, and like articles for birthday and other presents, with the whole list of accessories in the line of presentation goods and fancy nick-nacks.*

'*An important department comprises musical instruments, a large selection of high-class stringed instruments, both old and new, and many of them his own make, being*

kept on hand. The trade in these is always considerable, and is on the increase. Another department is devoted to relief stamping, general printing and engraving. Wedding, dance and mourning cards also form a speciality, and are supplied at the shortest notice and in the best style. The proprietor gives personal attention to the business, and a large connection throughout the district, among residents and visitors, is enjoyed. First-class wares at strictly moderate prices distinguish the establishment, and orders receive prompt attention. A 'Circulating Library' is a speciality and as this is connected with Mudie's of London, all the latest books are available for residents and visitors, a benefit specially advantageous to the latter.'

F.W. WOOLWORTH & Co. Ltd Bazaar

240 Whitley Road.

Founded by an American, Frank Winfield Woolworth in 1878, the first Woolworth store came to Whitley Bay in the mid 1920s. The original single-storey shop was situated next door to the former Council Chambers on Whitley Road which were demolished in 1955. Woolworths was then rebuilt over the site as a 3-storey building, and remained there until its closure in 2008.

R. SOUTHERN

Saddler, 257 Whitley Road.
Proprietor Ralph Southern.

Listed in a 1911 directory, amongst many of the other trades and businesses, Ralph Southern was a saddler and cobbler whose premises were situated almost opposite the Victoria (Vic) Hotel on Whitley Road.

E.H. ASKEW

Grocers and Provision Merchants,
265 Whitley Road.
Proprietor Mr Edmund H. Askew.
Re-numbered as 299 Whitley Road, trading as William Hill Bookmakers in 2016.

E.H. Askews grocery shop was a well-established business which stood for many years close to the corner of Whitley Road (Regent Street) and Laburnum Avenue. Generally known as 'Regent Stores', the name was taken from the stone plaque above the shop indicating 'Regent Street' (see page 14).

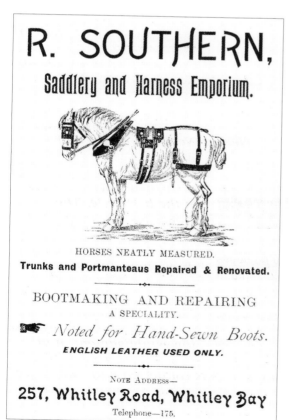

R.J. WILES

Confectioner & Pork Butcher, 272, 274, 276 Whitley Road.
Proprietor Mr Robert J. Wiles.

Robert Wiles was a butcher who ran a successful business throughout the 1920s. Apart from these shops situated on Whitley Road, next door to the Fat Ox Hotel, he also had premises situated at No. 17a Park Avenue and also Whitley Park Terrace on the seafront.

Tel 379 — Whitley Bay.

□ □

The popular Shops for Savouries, Veal, Ham & Pork Pies.

□ □

Pressed Beef, Tongues, Cheeks, etc.

□ □

NOTED FOR FRESH CREAM CAKES.

R. J. WILES, *High-class Confectioner, Pastrycook & Pork Purveyor,*
272, 274, 276 Whitley Road & 17a Park Avenue, Whitley Bay.

WHITLEY BAY
CO-OPERATIVE STORE

Grocery Store, Hardware and House Furnishers, 271 Whitley Road.
Re-numbered as 305 Whitley Road, which in 2016 was lying vacant.

Whitley Bay was once served by several branches of the North Shields Co-operative Society (founded in 1860) and opened its first Whitley Bay shop in 1902 as the North Shields Industrial Society. The premises, with its impressive curved frontage, were built on the corner of Whitley Road and Marden Road at the north east extremity of the former grounds of Whitley Hall.

At the beginning of the 1900s, local co-operators were not satisfied with having to trade either at Cullercoats or the North Shields branches, as a consequence of which, the management were repeatedly informed that unless a Whitley Bay branch was opened, one of two things would happen: a) a Whitley society would be formed or b) one of the other neighbouring societies would be invited to come into the area.

Influenced by these alternatives, the above site was purchased and opened with due ceremonial on 25th November 1902. From that day, the Co-op really never looked back on Whitley Bay and over the years there have been remarkable developments.

In 1944, when the society's plans for post-war expansion were laid, a chemists shop in Marden Road was purchased to become the drug department of the society.

In July 1946, grocery premises were acquired in Ilfracombe Gardens and in September of that year a mantles department was added to the Whitley Bay premises.

In June 1947, another large step was taken when the Co-op bought up the property of Barry Noble, a huge fruit and vegetable merchant which stood next to the former Woolworths store on Whitley Road. This was perhaps the most expensive of the society's post-war purchases, however, it soon paid back in dividends to its members, more than the cost of the business and property.

In October 1947, the purchase of another block of property led to the establishment of a separate society, North Shields Co-operative Chemists Ltd. A ladies hairdressing establishment was opened in December of the same year and June 1948 saw the opening of a florists shop and later a branch grocery store and butchers shop at the corner of Seatonville Road and Canberra Avenue, West Monkseaton. This long list of developments along with an even longer one in North Shields itself lifted sales from £272,000 in 1939 to £1,235,280 in 1952. Other services provided were a particularly good milk trade, with many of the deliveries once carried out by horse and cart.

At its peak, and every July, these animals were dressed and assembled for a carnival which became a regular sight in the area with a procession along the seafront from North Shields to Whitley Bay.

The Co-operative celebrated its centenary in 1960 and the sales target for that year was fixed at £2million.

Over 80% of the North Shields societies purchases were made from Co-op sources and in 1960, almost £100,000 was paid out in dividends. A truly successful story from humble beginnings.

In later years, branch stores were disbanded, and were nationally rebranded simply as the Co-op. as a result, the store on Whitley Road was vacated in 2010 and the premises relocated to a site opposite the former bus station on Park Avenue.

CROFTONS CAFÉ

Crofton's was a large café that was situated on Whitley Road, and a descriptive guidebook dated 1901 colourfully describes the premises as follows: *'This well-known café is situated within three minutes of the railway station, and about halfway between Whitley and Cullercoats. The building has a frontage of about twenty feet and is fitted up in a tastefully appropriate fashion, with marble tables, ottomans and chairs ornamented with plants which comprise a well arranged tea-room, well provided with lavatories and retiring rooms for ladies and gentlemen. Cyclists are able to leave their machines in the care of a male attendant, there being excellent accommodation*

provided. The stock is of the best of its kind, and includes all the leading makes of confectionery and chocolates – Cadbury's and Fry's.

'Since their establishment, a very good and increasing trade has been done, the shop supplying what may be described as a 'long-felt want' of the community. The tea, coffee, chocolate and other prepared refreshments are all that can be desired. The 'stores' which adjoin, have an attractive double frontage, and make an excellent display in the various lines of groceries and provisions. Prices in all departments are strictly moderate, and a large and efficient staff ensures the prompt execution of all orders placed in their hands. The headquarters of the firm are in Blackett Street, Newcastle, from which centre a large and active trade is carried on in distributing to the communities named, such necessary articles as are required.'

MRS M.E. SHEPHERD
Tobacconist, Newsagent, Stationer, Hairdresser and Confectioner, Whitley Road.

This business was run by a Mrs Marion Shepherd and eloquently described in 1901 as follows: *'A considerable diversity of vocations carried on at the establishment noted are above, Mrs Shepherd serving the public in a most effective manner as tobacconist, confectioner, purveyor of news and general information and amusement, dealer in all kinds of general and ornamental stationery and hairdresser. The shop is in the chief business thoroughfare of the town, near the railway station and every way convenient. There is a double frontage and a neat assortment of wares are displayed, including all the best brands of tobaccos, cigars and cigarettes, with the usual accessories in the line of pipes, pouches etc. The news department is carefully and energetically managed, daily and weekly newspapers with current magazines and periodicals being regularly supplied when desired. A very nice and up to date stock of stationery is kept, and hairdressing, shaving etc are carried on in a separate room in the back. Altogether the shop is a great convenience to the district.'*

MESSRS C. PHILLIPS & Co.

(Late Mrs Emily Thew), Booksellers, Stationers etc, 'The Library', Whitley Road.

A description of this business taken from a 1901 guidebook is as follows: 'The indispensable requisite of a good booksellers shop and stationery emporium is provided in Whitley by the establishment of C. Phillips & Co., in Whitley Road. The 'Library' is centrally and conveniently situated in the main business thoroughfare of the town, the premises being well adapted for the various lines carried on. A large and comprehensive stock of popular and select books is maintained in the circulating library, which is a recognised boon to the residents of the district and to visitors as well. There is also a remarkably good assortment of books for sale, including bibles, prayer books, hymn and tune books for 'Ancient and Modern', the hymnal companion etc. A large and varied supply of plain and fancy stationery, with the usual accessories of the trade, is also kept

on hand. Mention should also be made of the lines of general fancy goods, purses, frames, pocket books, leather articles and the like, which form an important branch of the establishment. Very superior table glass and china are supplied as well. The connection is well established and steadily growing, the business being under the immediate control of the proprietors. Orders in every department are promptly attended to.'

THE WHITLEY PUBLIC SALE ROOM

Whitley Road. Proprietor Mr George Bennion.

The Whitley public saleroom was situated on the south west side of Whitley Road, just a few yards from the junction with Victoria Terrace. A business descriptive from a 1901 guidebook is as follows: 'One of the greatest conveniences in a growing community is a place where sales of general household and other effects are regularly of frequently held, and Whitley fortunately possesses one in the establishment noted above, of which Mr George Bennion is the proprietor. The premises are conveniently situated, nearly opposite the Assembly Rooms, and daily sales are held of all the various classes of articles useful

to householders who are either giving up their homes or are desirous of furnishing anew. Mr Bennion is an expert in all matters pertaining to the business, and persons wishing to realise good prices for any superfluous articles in their possession cannot do better than place them in his hands. The business done at the room is of a various character, and almost any article possessing a saleable value may be obtained or disposed of there. Prompt attention is paid to all communications. Sales conducted on the most reasonable terms. Prompt settlements.'

PARK VIEW

At one time, Whitley Road continued through the village, past St Paul's Church, as far as the junction with Norham Road where it curved to the right and continued to the junction with Marine Avenue. At the bend of the road there was a short section sub-named Cartington Place. In 1926, the section between St Paul's Church and Norham Road junction was widened by 15 feet and towards the end of the 1930s, had been renamed as Park View in its entirety.

Part of the road widening scheme involved the demolition of the rectory wall of St Paul's Church which once extended as far as the present junction with Kings Drive.

The 1925 image below looks east along Whitley Road (Park View) towards St Paul's Church where the old rectory wall is visible to the right. The present shops were built in the 1930s and now occupy this land. To the left, a sign indicating Smith's Coronation Coal Depot is fixed to the projecting stone wall on the left and the lych-gate of St Paul's Church can be seen in the distance.

Whitley Road (Park View) prior to road widening work in 1926. Demolition of St Paul's Rectory is already underway. This view was taken from the corner next to Norham Road. The edge of the former Gas Board buildings are just visible to the right.

STEEL'S GARDENS

George Steel was born in 1849 at Barmoor Castle, Northumberland and by 1880 he had moved to Heatherslaw, a small constablewick situated between Etal and Ford Villages. Around 1901, George Steel, along with his wife Sarah and two sons from his first marriage, Joseph William and Richard moved from Heatherslaw to Whitley Bay where they established a successful business on Whitley Road (now Park View) as Market Gardeners, Nurserymen, Seedsmen and Florists, specialising in all manner of floristry and horticulture.

The land was collectively known as Percy Gardens (not to be confused with a street of the same name), and was leased from the Duke of Northumberland. Surrounded by a stone wall, the gardens occupied the area comprising all the present shops opposite St Paul's Church, to the boundary with back Roxburgh Terrace, and the area known as Northumberland Square (to the rear of the Fat Ox), which included the land previously occupied by the former bus station.

Several greenhouses existed within these gardens, and George Steel introduced a heating system whereby hot water pipes were placed inside the old flues of the wall which bounded the rear of the gardens to provide additional heat to these and other outhouses. One of the larger greenhouses was used as an indoor vineyard to grow grapes.

In 1911, George also purchased a large area of land, along with four cottages at West Park, Hillheads from the descendants of a Richard Heckels Nesbitt who was the previous owner. This land originally formed the north western edge of Whitley Limestone Quarry, and stood adjacent to the present Ice Rink.

(More reading about the Steel family and West Park in *Monkseaton Village – Volume 2* published by Summerhill Books.)

G. STEEL & SON

Nurserymen, Seedsmen, and Florists.

WHITLEY GARDENS
(Opposite St. Paul's Church),

WHITLEY BAY.

GARDEN SEEDS - A large and choice selection of Flower and Vegetable Seeds always in stock. Bedding-out Plants a Speciality. Choice Cut Flowers and Vegetables from own garden. Table Plants, Bouquets, Wreaths, and other Floral Designs made to order. Gardens attended to and estimates given for every class of work. Experienced Workmen sent out.

SPECIAL LINES - Grapes, Tomatoes, Cucumbers, Salads, early Potatoes, and Cut Flowers.

INSPECTION INVITED.

Steel's Gardens were situated on Whitley Road (Park View), opposite St Paul's Church. The entrance to the gardens is indicated by a sign above the door of his residence (No. 288 Whitley Road), shown in this picture. The church lych-gate is to the right, and the Co-op store can be seen in the background.

For a time, George and his family took up residence at 288 Whitley Road, a large house, which stood directly next to the Fat Ox Hotel, and adjoined the gardens. The gardens were managed by George along with his two sons, Joseph and Richard, where the business flourished until 1923 when much of the land was sold by the Duke of Northumberland for retail development. 288 Whitley Road was later demolished and is now occupied by the present shops and the newer Shopping Mall. A small section of the nursery gardens remained to the rear of Roxburgh Terrace and the former bus station until the mid-1950s.

Left to right: Joseph, William and George Steel. The photograph was taken in the gardens opposite St Paul's Church.

Whitley Road (Park View) undergoing widening work in the 1920s. The stone wall enclosing Steel's gardens has been demolished, and the rectory wall of St Paul's Church is still intact, prior to the present shops being built.

PARK VIEW SHOPS

EAMES ART SHOP
Art Dealer & Picture Framer, 288 Whitley Road. Proprietor Mr Leonard F. Eames.
Re-numbered as 20 Park View, trading as Natwest Bank in 2016

When Steel's Gardens ceased trading during the 1920s to make way for the present shops, Mr Leonard Eames opened his art dealership and picture framing business here about 1932. At that time, the shop was situated at the end of the new block. The building is still intact, but has undergone significant alteration work to the frontage where in 2016 it was trading as Natwest Bank.

T. DUNN
Fish Merchant & Poulterer, 307 Whitley Road. Proprietor Mr Thomas Dunn & Sons.
Re-numbered as 111 Park View, trading as Sunlight Cleaners in 2016.

The first record of Thomas Dunn's business appears in a Ward's Directory dated 1911-12. The business became well established in the town and was still trading until at least 1940 Mr. Dunn also had a further branch of the business situated at 13 Front Street, Monkseaton.

BAINBRIDGE & Co.

House Furnishers, 328 & 330 Whitley Road.
Re-numbered as 80 & 82 Park View.

The image below looks east along Park View (Whitley Road) and shows Bainbridge's furniture and carpet showroom to the left. The building with the large apexed roof next to the protruding stone wall still exists, and bears a terracotta plaque dated 1892 on the upper frontage, however the buildings towards camera were later demolished and replaced by the curved corner frontage which formed part of Ryle's ladies fashion shop.

FINLAY & SONS

Decorators & Signwriters, 331 Whitley Road. Proprietor Mr John Finlay.
Re-numbered as 125 Park View.

First established at Blyth in 1908 by a Mr John Finlay, the Whitley Bay branch at No. 331 Whitley Road (Park View) was opened in 1931 and has continued trading in the town ever since. The company is now one of the oldest established businesses in Whitley Bay. A further shop was opened in August 1936, at No. 24 Front Street, Tynemouth, but ceased trading after just two years in July 1938.

All sign writing work was carried out by Mr John Henderson Finlay (Jack), son of the founder, who was responsible for much of the painted advertising signage usually seen on the gable-ends of many buildings in the area during the early to mid 20th century. Some of his other notable work included sign writing on the local Hunter's Buses. The image below was taken on Duke Street, Whitley Bay, just around the corner from their original premises, with Park View visible to the background. Although the signage on the van indicates their address as 331 Park View, it was in fact 331 Whitley Road, which later became Park View. By 1934, Finlay's moved to new premises situated at 292 Whitley Road, (Now No. 28 Park View), opposite St Paul's Church, where the business still continues to run under family ownership.

36

RYLE'S

Fashion and Milliners, 340 Whitley Road. Proprietor Madame Sarah Ryle.
Re-numbered as 84 Park View.

Perhaps one of the most well-known shops in Whitley Bay in more recent years was Ryle's fashions. Its history goes back to 1911 when it was just a small one-windowed shop which was first opened by Mrs Sarah Ryle to sell high quality hats, skirts and blouses. There was nothing flamboyant about the premises as it was tucked away between a dairy and a furniture shop.

When rebuilding work took place on Park View during the late 1920s, Ryle's fashions remained in the same location, however it was reconstructed as a prominent three-storey block to occupy a prominent corner site on Park View. The business expanded rapidly and once boasted a total of 20 departments selling furs to swimsuits and coats to babywear. The business also hosted two fashion shows each year during the Spring and Autumn months.

Sarah Ryle died in 1939 and the shop continued trading as a family business until its eventual closure in the 1970s. Part of the premises later became a fitness centre known as Ivy Court, and has since been occupied by a number of other retail businesses over the years.

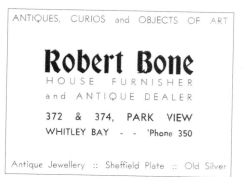

ANTIQUES, CURIOS and OBJECTS OF ART

Robert Bone
HOUSE FURNISHER
and ANTIQUE DEALER

372 & 374, PARK VIEW
WHITLEY BAY - - 'Phone 350

Antique Jewellery :: Sheffield Plate :: Old Silver

ROBERT BONE

Furniture Dealer, 372 & 374 Whitley Road.
Re-numbered as 114 & 116 Park View, trading as a
sandwich shop and a pharmacy in 2016.

The first record of Robert Bone's shop appears in a trades directory dated 1920. Although listings show his business as a furniture dealer, it is however quite evident from the picture that he also dealt in jewellery, antiques and silverware. The business continued at these premises, which were situated on the corner of Park View and Park Parade until at least 1940

C. NICHOLSON

Butcher, 396 Whitley Road.
Proprietor Mr Charles Nicholson.
Re-numbered as 140 Park View.

In 1914, Charles Nicholson established his butchers shop at No. 396 Whitley Road (140 Park View). This shop is the last remaining traditional independent family butcher in Whitley Bay and is one of the town's longest established businesses.

The business eventually passed to Charles Nicholson's son (also named Charles). The business has since passed on and is now run and managed by the third and fourth generation of this well-known local family which in 2014, celebrated 100 years of existence, with the shop continuing to trade from the very same premises that it was first established in.

Doug Nicholson, grandson of the founder Charles Nicholson.

M. WHITE

Stationer, 409 Whitley Road. Proprietor Mrs M. White.
Re-numbered as 207 Park View, trading as a Dog Groomers in 2016.

The only listings for this business appear in Trade Directories dated 1926 and 1928

where it is recorded as a stationers shop, however as indicated on the picture it would appear that it also incorporated a confectioner and tobacconist. There is however no reference to the ladies and gents hairdressing rooms as indicated on the signboard which were probably located on the upper floor of the premises.

Originally numbered as 409 Whitley Road, and situated at the very end of the street, close to the corner with Marine Avenue, it had been re-numbered as 207 Park View by 1938.

J.C. FEATONBY

Estate Agent, Auctioneer and Valuer, Whitley Road. Proprietor Mr John C. Featonby.
Re-numbered as 234-236 Park View.

Featonby's auction rooms situated on Park View are well known in the area, and have been established in the town since the mid-1930s, however their early history is somewhat vague. Between 1897 and 1920, Trade Directories show a solicitor by the name of Augustus Whitehorn practising from Egremont Place, Whitley Bay. By 1926, this name appears to be linked to a firm of estate agents located at 404 Whitley Road and operating under the name of Whitehorn & Featonby. In 1928, the same firm is listed at 426a Whitley Road.

By 1930, the company had moved to No. 448 Whitley Road where they traded as Whitehorn & Featonby (Estate Agents, Auctioneers and Valuers). By 1936, it appears

that this business had closed and according to trades directories of the period, a John Charlton Featonby acquired new premises on Whitley Road (now renumbered as 234-236 Park View) where he established a new business operating as J.C. Featonby and became an estate agent for the Halifax Building Society in Whitley Bay. At this time, the premises consisted of two separate shops: 234 Park View were the auction rooms and 236 was a builders office run by a J.F. Featonby.

It would appear that sometime after the 1940s, the builders business ceased and the premises were merged into one to run as auctioneers and valuers. The upstairs sale room was added in the 1960s and the first antique sale was held there on 26th November 1962.

The business has been family-run ever since with the ground floor shop frontage still retaining almost all of its original features.

STATION ROAD

Station Road was the main street running between Whitley Railway Station and Whitley Road, beyond which it connected with the Esplanade, which over the years has led countless thousands of visitors towards the promenade and beach at the height of the holiday season. In 1888 a group of gentlemen met with the intention of having a meeting place built that would rival anything else found in the area. A site was identified on the corner of Whitley Road and Station Road and building work commenced on what was to become the Whitley & District Club Co. Ltd. The finished structure incorporated a clock built into a corner dormer on the upper floor and an under-archway leading off Station Road to allow access into a rear lane. The scheme was slow to start, as a result of which, parts of the premises had to be let out. As a result, it was in 1895 when James Young opened a fashionable drapers store on the ground floor, which later became Young and Aiston, and then Aiston & Son followed by W.J. Sparkes as shown on the photograph below. Around the First World War, the premises were taken over by Lloyds Bank and in more recent years, the lower floor became a restaurant and the upper floor became the Whitley Bay Coast Club.

Taken from the junction with Whitley Road, this busy street view of Station Road dates to around 1908. Whitley Railway Station can be seen in the distance (minus the clock-tower) which was not added until 1910.

STATION ROAD SHOPS

All these premises still exist but the businesses are long gone and, over the years, many of the original shop frontages have been altered or replaced.

Mr T. THOMPSON

House Furnisher and Upholsterer, 2 Station Road. Proprietor Mr Thomas Thompson.

Thomas Thompson was a house furnisher and upholsterer with premises situated in Newcastle and at No. 2 Station Road, Whitley Bay. A descriptive taken from a 1901 guidebook to the town describes the business as follows: '*An indispensable adjunct in any growing community, seaside or inland, is an establishment for supplying house furnishing*

requirements, and the rapidly developing resort of Whitley-by-the-Sea is fortunately provided for in this respect. Mr T. Thompson is familiar with the trade in all its branches, and his shop in Station Road is supplied with all the articles necessary for the complete furnishing of houses great and small. The stock is of a comprehensive character, and includes the usual articles of furniture, dining-room, drawing-room and bed-room suites and the like, with an excellent assortment of carpets, floorcloths, linoleums and general furnishing materials. Any class of goods in the trade not on hand can be procured expeditiously, and prompt attention is given to all orders and commissions.

A large and continuously extending trade is done in Whitley and the district, the house being well known for good management and fair dealing.'

WILLIAM PATTINSON

Dealer in Glass, China and Art ware, etc, Station Road.

Extract from a 1901 guidebook: '*A very neat and comprehensive stock of glass, china, earthenware, art ware etc, is offered by Mr William Pattinson, at the above address in*

Whitley. The shop, which is built of brick and has a good double frontage, is near the railway station, a handsome stock being at all times maintained in the lines noted. Flower vases, plant pots, flower bowls, tea sets, and a host of useful and ornamental articles in the wares mentioned are offered at surprisingly low figures, the high artistic quality of the different pieces being a marked feature. Mr Pattinson has access to the best markets, and the excellence of his judgment is manifest in his selection of wares. A steadily-growing trade is done in the town and district, the public recognising the sterling character of the goods handled, and greatly appreciating the bargains which are constantly offered to purchasers. A special selection of various articles in china with views of Whitley, Cullercoats and Tynemouth.'

GLADSTONE ADAMS

In 1904 Gladstone Adams opened up a studio at No. 18 Station Road, Whitley Bay and became a notable photographer in the district, as well as becoming a great producer of local picture postcards. His premises were situated on the corner of Albany Gardens

and still exist, having changed hands a number of times over the years. Soon after the end of the Second World War, the business transferred from Station Road studio to his home at 11 Beverley Park, Monkseaton.

Gladstone Adams was born at Newcastle in 1880, and after serving an initial apprenticeship with Tynemouth photographer, Matthew Auty, he set up his own photographic business in Barras Bridge, Newcastle before transferring to Station Road.

Gladstone Adams received recognition when in 1908, he drove his motor car to Crystal Palace to watch his beloved Newcastle United Football Club play Wolverhampton Wanderers in the FA Cup Final. On his way home, having endured the 3-1 defeat of his team, snow kept obscuring the car windscreen and he regularly had to stop to manually clean it. This frustrating experience inspired the invention of the windscreen wiper, the design of which he eventually patented in 1911. His version however was never actually manufactured, and in the history books it is an American who is actually credited with the invention. Adam's prototype however, can been seen on display in Newcastle's Discovery Museum.

Adams became a local councillor, and later chairman of Whitley Bay Urban District Council. During the First World War, he served in the Royal Flying Corps (the forerunner of the RAF), as a photographic reconnaissance officer. He attained the title of Captain, and one of his duties was to prove the death and then arrange the burial of Baron Manfred von Richthofen alias 'The Red Baron', after he had been shot down and killed. Adams died in 1966 at his home in Monkseaton.

WHITLEY RAILWAY STATION

In 1864, the Blyth and Tyne Railway Company built a track to its terminus at Tynemouth, bypassing the then small community of Whitley Village. The very first Whitley Station actually stood on the site of what is now Souter Park, Monkseaton. When the North Eastern Railway Company took over the Blyth and Tyne Railway in 1874, plans were laid out for a loop to link the expanding coastal communities to the network. The line which opened in July 1882 follows the same route as the current Metro system.

In 1902, the company considered tenders for the electrification of the line and trial runs from Newcastle to Tynemouth took place in February 1904 and via Whitley Bay in May that year. By the end of 1904, it was announced that electric express trains would run to and from Newcastle.

The railway station itself was small and cramped, and so construction work commenced in 1908 on a new Renaissance style building which still stands to this day. The building was designed by a Mr W. Bell. The impressive clock tower was added in 1910 as a central feature to complete the façade symmetry and stands prominently overlooking Station Road.

Over the years, the railway brought thousands of visitors and holidaymakers to Whitley, all of whom had a short straight walk to the seaside and beach via Station Road and The Esplanade.

Returning after a visit to the seaside, crowds of day-trippers queue up in an orderly manner outside Whitley Bay Railway Station.

In 1889, Thomas Harvey was the station master and was awarded a biscuit box as a prize for his excellence in keeping the adjoining station gardens, and even as late as 1969, the station was still winning prizes for its cleanliness and decorations.

Just a few yards away from the main station entrance (close to the corner with Clarence Crescent), stands a very rare telephone kiosk which incorporates a telephone, letterbox and a coin-operated machine for issuing postage stamps. Introduced in 1928, and known as a 'Type K4', less than 50 of these kiosks were installed throughout the country, however they proved to be unpopular with customers, and as such, the majority were withdrawn in 1935 but somehow this one managed to survive, eventually becoming Grade II listed in October 1986.

LABURNUM AVENUE

Soon after Whitley Hall was demolished in 1899, Laburnum Avenue was laid out by Alfred Styan, a pioneer builder in Whitley Bay. An ornate dated stone plaque is still evident on the last building towards the end of the road near its junction with Regent Street (Whitley Road).

Unlike most streets in the area, which have odd numbers to one side and even numbers opposite, Laburnum Avenue is consecutively numbered on both sides of the street.

WHITLEY BAY POLICE STATION
20-24 Laburnum Avenue.

Occupying a site within the former grounds of Whitley Hall (see page 12), Whitley Bay Police Station was built on Laburnum Avenue in 1902, along with the surrounding streets which comprise Victoria Terrace, Jesmond Terrace, Clifton Terrace, Fern Avenue, The Crescent and Crescent Vale.

Very little information exists in relation to the Police building, the decorative frontage of which is constructed from smooth engineering bricks. A neat row of wrought iron railings once enclosed a small and narrow garden area to the front and south side which extended around the corner into Fern Avenue.

This was an important building which incorporated two courtrooms and offices for Magistrates clerks and court staff on the first floor. Carved stones are evident above the front entrance doors indicating entrances for Magistrates and the Public.

Interestingly, in the early 1930s, the house situated at No. 9 Laburnum Avenue (which stood opposite the Police Station) had been commissioned as the office for the Clerk to the Justices, and for a number of years, the Juvenile Court sessions were held there. The ground floor of the actual police station however, consisted of a public counter, parade room, offices and interview rooms, along with a CID department. Cells were centrally situated towards the rear of the building where a prisoners entrance and yard was located.

Housing accommodation was incorporated within the Police Station and this was situated to the rear of the building, which in the early days was once the residence of the Inspector and Sergeant-in-charge. Over the years however, this arrangement was dispensed with, as a result of which, the housing blocks were altered to become offices.

Technically – the Police Station and its buildings were numbered 20-24 Laburnum Avenue.

M. HEWITT

Office and Bakery, 25 and 26 Laburnum Avenue. Proprietor Mr Mark Hewitt.

Mark Hewitt's bakery and head office were situated at Nos. 25 and 26 Laburnum Avenue, directly next door to Whitley Bay Police Station. The building later became better known to many people as John W. Welch, sweet manufacturer. The 1920s advertisement below proclaims Hewitt's cafés and dairies, which were situated at 153 Whitley Road, 12 East Parade and 9 Park Terrace, 10 Spanish City and 98 West Percy Street at North Shields. The image shown on the advertisement is probably that of their premises situated at 9 Park Terrace, Whitley Bay. (Now demolished as part of the seafront regeneration scheme.)

JOHN W. WELCH LTD
Toffee Manufacturers, 26 Laburnum Avenue.

The smaller building which adjoined the police station to the north, was originally M. Hewitt's bakery, which in the early 1930s was taken over by John W. Welch, a local sweet and toffee manufacturer and became locally known as 'The Toffery'.

Welch's were a family-run business with a large factory at Norham Road, North Shields run by Mr Tom Welch where the main production line was mostly packaged sweets. The smaller premises at Whitley Bay however, were run by Tom Welch's brother who produced the old-fashioned type of sweets that were usually sold separately by weight from large glass jars in confectioners shops.

It is claimed that he invented 'Black Bullets' and dark rolled mints, but it was in fact toffee that Welch's were renowned for – Plain Toffee, Treacle Toffee, Liquorice Toffee and so on, Welch's were famous for the stuff!

The ornate North Shields branch of John W. Welch which was situated at 18 Russell Street in the 1930s.

Production ran there almost on a daily basis and the smell of sweet toffee often filled the air around the neighbouring streets. The business continued at this location for well over 50 years before the company vacated the building during the 1990s. It was later purchased by Northumbria Police Authority as additional storage space.

WILF HEWISON
Gentlemens Hairdresser, 31 Laburnum Avenue.

In 1935, Wilfred Hewison began a gentlemen's hairdressing business with premises that were situated at No. 31 Laburnum Avenue, close to the corner with Regent Street (Whitley Road).

By 1940, he had transferred to No. 63 Front Street, Monkseaton where he also combined the business with a newsagency, and up to the 1960s, continued his hairdressing trade in the back of the shop.

YORK ROAD

York Road lies within the presumed extent of Whitley medieval village which was a gift of Henry I to Tynemouth Priory. Whitley was once a two-row village, perhaps with a green and a hall in the centre of the south side.

In 1539, it is known that there were only five copyhold tenants in the village, each with a tenement and piece of land. There was also a cottage and an orchard. Today the site of the medieval village lies around the crossroads of Park View, Whitley Road and Marden Road. York Road however marks the former line of the back lane of the medieval village.

This old cottage on York Road served as a depot for the local council. The officials shown here are from left to right: the Road Foreman, Mr Purvis, Mr Thomas Thompson of Hillheads Farm, Mr Mather and the Urban District Surveyor, Mr Moore. The portly man standing in the doorway is the hackmaster, Mr Robert James Wilkin.

THE FIRE STATION

Whitley Bay's first fire station was built in 1890, immediately next to the York Road cottages. It was rebuilt in 1908 at a cost of £3,000, by William Gray of Park Parade to become the new headquarters of the Whitley Bay and Monkseaton Fire Brigade.

The building had accommodation for five of the 12 full-time firemen and their families, as well as a duty room, workshops and a stable for four horses which pulled a Merryweather steam-powered pumping engine. The fire crew later became responsible for the town ambulance which was also garaged behind the main building.

Following government reorganisation, the Fire Station closed in 1991 and the building was later purchased by the J.D. Wetherspoon pub chain for conversion into a large public house, retaining the name as 'The Fire Station'.

The exterior of the building remains generally intact with minimal alterations.

PARK AVENUE AND PARK ROAD

The parcel of land known as Whitley Park (Refer to *Whitley Bay Remembered – Part 1*), loaned its name to Park Avenue and Park Road. Before the housing which now comprises Roxburgh Terrace, Park Parade, Beach Avenue, Holly Avenue, Coquet Avenue and Marine Gardens was built, the park would have been visible from the main shopping street which assumed the obvious and appropriate name of Park View.

WHITLEY DAIRY FARM

Whitley Dairy Farm stood near the top of Park Avenue on the site of what later became the General Post Office and Bus Station. During the 17th century, much of the village of Whitley belonged to the prominent Hudson family from whom it descended through the Ellisons and Bensons, eventually coming into the possession of a North Shields Shipowner, William Davison in 1855.

Davison owned other land at Preston, Monkseaton and Whitley and also ran a butchering business in the Low Town of North Shields, raising his own cattle to supply the business as well as supplying meat provisions to ships. This farm was inherited by his son, John Davison and in the 1880s was placed under the management of a James Ord and later by Henry Davison Hickey when it was often referred to as Hickeys Dairy Farm. During Henry Hickey's tenancy, the land was sold off and the first buildings to be erected on the land were St Edward's Church and School. By 1907, streets and housing were also laid out which included Roxburgh Terrace, Park Parade, Beach Avenue, Holly Avenue and Coquet Avenue.

A worn sandstone date plaque is visible on the upper level of the corner building of Roxburgh Terrace indicating the year of construction. The Post Office was not built until 1925 and in 1935 United Automobile Services acquired the remaining farm buildings and cleared the site to make way for a new bus station.

Hickeys Farm, Park Avenue c.1907, looking north. The Post Office and Bus Station later occupied this site.

50

Above: Hickeys Farm, Park Avenue c.1907, looking south towards the corner of Whitley Road and the former Ship Hotel which is also visible on the photograph. Roxburgh Terrace was laid out to the immediate left of these buildings.

Right: The worn sandstone date plaque at the end of Roxburgh Terrace.

F.E. MAUGHAN

In 1934, Seaton Sluice house builder, Frank Edward Maughan, took over a vacant site at Benton in order to store and manufacture the range of materials he needed to construct properties. The market expanded, and two years later Frank decided to purchase town centre premises in Park Avenue, Whitley Bay, to store smaller items of hardware together with the various plumbing materials he needed for his building activities. After the store opened, he immediately tapped into a local demand for small hardware products such as locks and other small items and was quickly obliged to introduce a counter service. As an instinctive business man with a nose for new opportunities, Frank saw the potential for his business to supply others, both trade and public. At the outbreak of the Second World War in 1939, housebuilding virtually disappeared from the agenda throughout Britain. Soon after the start of hostilities, the government made compulsory use of the company's building materials site at Benton, to store timber and supplies to repair bomb damaged properties and therefore Frank was obliged to 'bank' on his new hardware store at Whitley Bay, until that is, a bomb dropped on nearby Ocean View, causing substantial damage his premises.

At the end of hostilities, the business at Benton was re-established and developed further with the introduction of a delivery service. Frank's son, Rowland, joined the company in 1954, and became managing director. Neighbouring shop premises in Park Avenue were later purchased and the whole retail hardware and plumbing operation expanded with the later addition of a separate department selling household goods, gifts and crafts.

Frank Edward Maughan, Founder.

In the early 1970s, the Park Avenue site was again upgraded with the addition of a two-storey retail and administration centre.

In 1982, after a fire had largely destroyed the Benton site the previous year, a new purpose built trading facility was established covering 16,000 square feet.

Frank Maughan died in 1976 but the business continues to be run as a family concern.

F.E. Maughan's premises has stood on the corner of Park Avenue and York Road, Whitley Bay since 1936.

Counter assistant, Jim Knott and Rowland Maughan c.1955.

WHITLEY BAY LIBRARY

Up to 1939, there was no public library in Whitley Bay and prior to that time, the expense of having one was strongly opposed, however after much soul-searching, the council managed to secure a lease above the bus station in Park Avenue, in which the first library was to be opened.

In April 1939, Miss Mary Wright was appointed as the first librarian, and at the time the local press made a big play of the fact that her salary would be the same as a second-year policeman. The library opened for business on 3rd January 1940, with around 6,000 volumes of books and by 1954, the number of books stocked had risen to over 25,000 whilst books issued for loan for that period amounted to 350,000.

In 1963, Whitley Council began planning for a new library and a site was chosen in Whitley Park. The new building opened in 1966, and the old bus station library closed to become a night spot, known by many as the 'Sands Club'.

Miss Wright continued in office until 1970 when she was replaced by Mr J.B. West. The library in Whitley Park closed in 2013 and was relocated in a new building situated in York Road, Whitley Bay.

Park Avenue and Whitley Park c.1900. When the library moved from the former bus station, it was relocated to Whitley Park, on the left, behind the trees in 1966. This view looks north east along Park Avenue towards the seafront.

TAYLORS GARAGE

Built in 1930 and situated on the corner of Park Road and Marine Gardens, the premises formerly known as 'Fowlers Garage' was acquired in 1959 by the already well established Monkseaton firm, Taylors Garage. This allowed expansion of the company and their Vauxhall dealership to provide sufficient room and additional workspace to accommodate an extra large showroom, service departments, plus paint and body shops. Taylors ceased trading in 1985, and the premises were taken over to be used for a while as the 'Spanish City Indoor Market'. By the late 1990s, the premises had fallen into disuse and were later demolished to provide a car parking area for the adjacent Whitley Bay Playhouse.

More information about Taylors Garage can be found in *Monkseaton Village – Volume 1*.

Taylors Garage, Park Road c.1980.

SOUTH PARADE

South Parade was originally laid out in the late 1800s and built up as a wide residential street of large and very stylish three storey houses, most of which were owned or occupied by some of the more affluent people of the town. All of these houses had walled gardens with ornamental wrought iron railings. In the 1920s, Whitley Bay's popularity as a seaside resort began to grow rapidly, as a result of which the owners of these houses saw the potential to supplement their income by letting out some of the rooms to holidaymakers who were staying in the area, and as such, it became quite a lucrative business. The

The Victorian beauty and charm of South Parade c.1902, at a time when it was a desirable and affluent street.

profits were good, and many of the owners therefore converted their premises into Guest Houses and Bed & Breakfast accommodation, specifically catering for guests and visitors. During the years up to 1950, many changes took place to these buildings and some of the owners began to expand their businesses by taking over adjacent properties, to convert them into larger 'mini-hotels'.

Some of the premises were subsequently granted liquor licences where guests and residents could purchase alcohol and drink in the comfort of the place they were staying. Some establishments were even permitted to open their doors to 'non-residents', and so the potential for sales of drink to the public grew. As a result, the numerous 'pubs', 'bars' and 'hotels' which occupied the street in later years, were simply a gradual migration from the original houses. The original metal railings and garden walls were demolished to make way for car parking areas and outside patios. Extra attic rooms were added, thus destroying much of the upper ornamental architecture and rooflines. Bay windows, doors and porches have been pulled out and replaced with garish modern frontages and signage.

By the early 1970s, South Parade had lost almost all of its original Victorian charm and character and now bears no resemblance whatsoever to its original magnificent splendour. As alterations still continue to this day, the identity of this once beautiful street was well and truly lost in favour of business development, most of which was marketed or branded with a series of modern theme bars and 'fun pubs'.

The Harlow Hotel, 26-28 South Parade in the 1950s. With all of its original architecture and a nicely cultivated front garden, this is a typical example of what many of the houses on the north side of the street once looked like. In more recent years, these premises became better known as the 'Avalon Hotel'.

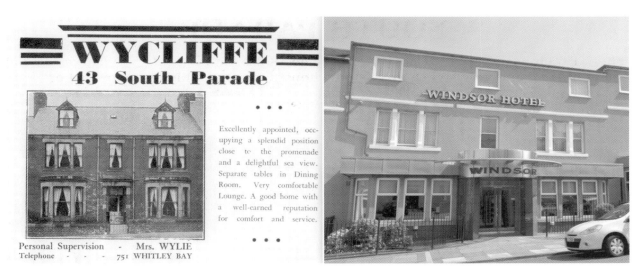

Above left: A 1930s advertisement shows the Wycliffe Hotel at No. 43 South Parade, Whitley Bay. This house has since been transformed into the Windsor Hotel (above right). It is difficult to believe this is the same building, as hardly any of the original features are evident apart from the triple windows to the first floor and the stone coping which marked the original roofline. This is a good example of how the architecture of the street has been transformed over the years as properties have been bought up for conversion into larger commercial premises.

EXCHANGE BUILDINGS

The Exchange Buildings which stand at the corner of South Parade and Oxford Street, were designed by a Mr William N. Scaife (architect) who also drew up plans for the prominent Central Hall situated on the opposite corner of South Parade and Whitley Road. The Exchange Buildings were originally commissioned by a Mr William Arthur Laws and the building contract was awarded to W.T. Weirs of Howdon on Tyne.
The colourful opening ceremony took place on 11th June 1910 with a performance by the then newly-formed Whitley Bay Military Band.

William Laws was originally a music teacher who sold musical instruments from premises in Station Road before setting up a business in 'Arcadia' on Whitley Road as a dealer in cycles, prams and electrical goods. After the new Exchange Buildings were opened, William Laws took four units of the building to open a 'Penny Bazaar', as well as selling Toys, Incandescent Mantles, Plumbing and Electrical Fittings, Cycles, Prams, Bathchairs, plus other hardware and domestic fittings. Other units were let out to a Mr Slater who sold paintings, a Mr Winter, Dairy Produce, a Mr Hall, Fruiterer and a Mrs Fulton who ran the Dainty café on the upper floor.

Laws also opened a motor garage to the rear of the premises on Oxford Street which operated under the name W.A. Laws & Co. Ltd where he became an agent selling and servicing Ford, Swift, Humber, Wolseley, Belsize and Detroiter cars.

Although having changed hands several times over the years, the garage is still in existence with very few external changes.

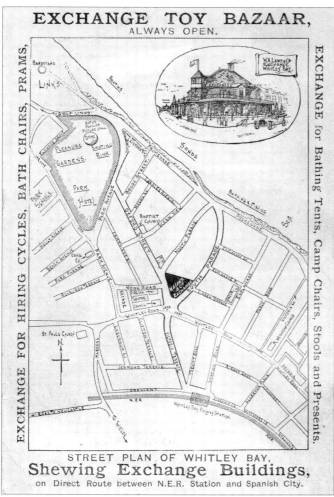

William Laws was a prominent figure in old Whitley and served as a councillor for 7 years until his death on 24th January 1931. He also served for a number of years on the Tynemouth Board of Guardians.

In later years, the Exchange buildings were taken over by Books Fashions, and during the 1960s the upstairs rooms became a night-spot which was well known as the 'Compass Club'.

In more recent years, the entire building underwent significant internal alteration work when it was converted to become a public house, better known today as Fitzgerald's. The typical character of the building has been retained with old Edwardian style windows and much of its original ornamental verandah to the frontage.

Laws Garage c.1924, situated on Oxford Street.

LAWS & Co., Ltd., Central Garage,

TAXICABS,
AUTOMOBILE ENGINEERS.

Repairs attended to without delay.   Any make of
Car Supplied. Driving & Running Repairs Taught.

Agents for

CITROEN,   GWYNNE,
ALBERT,   -   FORDS.

FORD Authorised Service and Agents. Taxis or
Touring Cars on Hire, with or without drivers.

Motorists should make Our Garage their Centre.

Local Runs on Private Cars.			
Rothbury	62m. £3	0	0
Alnwick	70m. £3	5	0
Chollerford	64m. £3	0	0
Wooler and			
Borders	100m. £5	0	0
Barnard Castle	100m. £5	0	0
Allendale	86m. £4	0	0
Bamburgh	104m. £5	0	0
Morpeth Bilsay			
Ponteland (Cir.)	45m. £2	5	0
Newcastle	20m. £1	0	0
Hexham	64m. £3	5	0
Durham	50m. £2	10	0

One hour waiting time included, or extra
time charged.   Above rates are for four
Passengers.   Refreshment houses on
each run.   Male or Female Drivers
as desired.

OXFORD ST.,   WHITLEY BAY.   'Phone 179.

A 1920s advertisement for W.A. Laws Garage, Oxford Street.

NORHAM ROAD

WHITLEY BAY MASONIC HALL

Whitley Bay Masonic Hall, is situated on the corner of Norham Road and Park View and was opened for the first time on 13th March 1913. The building was used by Freemasons for many years as a place to hold their respective Lodge Meetings.

On the evening of 8th December 1941 an air raid took place over Whitley Bay, and a number of enemy planes were engaged in an attack on the town, during which time a salvo of bombs was released, one of which fell into the centre of Norham Road completely destroying the Masonic Hall and

causing serious damage to neighbouring properties. As a result, temporary premises situated at No. 220 Whitley Road (Whitley Assembly Rooms), were hired, and all subsequent Masonic Meetings were held there for a number of years afterwards.

In 1954, building work commenced to replace the Masonic Hall with a new single storey building, which was designed by William Stockdale of North Shields.

Members of Whitley Lodge No. 2821, founded in October 1900. This image dates to c.1910.

The building was opened in October 1955 by the Provincial Grand Master for Northumberland, RW.Bro. J.M.S. Coates OBE, and all Masonic meetings at the coast resumed and continued to be held there up to the present day.

The two World Wars both had a great effect on English Freemasonry. Nationally, in the three years after the First World War over 350 new Lodges were set up, and in the three years after the Second World War nearly 600 new Lodges came into being. In many cases the founders were servicemen who wanted to continue the camaraderie they had built up during their war service, and were looking for a calm centre in a greatly changed and changing world.

Freemasonry in Whitley Bay was no exception and, over the years, up to 13 different Lodges and a number of other Masonic side orders have met in this hall, usually on a monthly basis with different meeting nights and large attendance figures. Many of these individual Lodges derived their names from localised places, such as Whitley Lodge, Monkseaton Lodge, St Mary's Lodge, BrierDene Lodge, Belvedere Lodge and Links Lodge.

Freemasonry is one of the world's oldest secular fraternal societies and is a society of men concerned with moral and spiritual values. Its members are taught its precepts (moral lessons and self-knowledge) by a series of ritual dramas – a progression of allegorical two-part plays which are learnt by heart and performed within each Lodge and which follow ancient forms, using stonemasons' customs and tools as allegorical guides. The Square and Compasses have therefore long been regarded as the universal symbols of Freemasonry.

Freemasonry instils in its members a moral and ethical approach to life: it seeks to reinforce thoughtfulness for others, kindness in the community, honesty in business, courtesy in society and fairness in all things. Members are urged to regard the interests of the family as paramount but, importantly, Freemasonry also teaches and practices concern for people, care for the less fortunate and help for those in need.

Inside Whitley Bay Masonic Hall.

WHITLEY NEW ROW

Whitley New Row was the name given to a row of white cottages which stood across the western end of Plessey Crescent on what is now Marden Road South.

In Tomlinson's History of Whitley, it is noted that Whitley New Row existed in 1867 however a census reference of 1841 suggests that under the name of 'Whitley Row', the cottages were inhabited mostly by miners, probably from the nearby Whitley Colliery. Inhabitants of the cottages appear in directories up to 1936, however by 1938, Whitley New Row no longer appeared on the Ordnance Survey Maps and had been demolished.

These views look south from Marden Road, towards the Broadway and were taken from a point close to the present Marden Bridge.

PUBLIC HOUSES

THE FAT OX

The Fat Ox takes its name from the animal which was immortalised by Thomas Bewick. Bewick was an artist and engraver who specialised in natural history, and was renowned for his illustrated History of British Birds as well as those images featured in Aesop's Fables. Bewick often worked in partnership with Ralph Beilby and had a workshop at Amen Corner in Newcastle. It is without doubt that one of Bewick's most famous illustrations was that of a massive ox, which was owned by Edward Hall, of Whitley Park Hall and reared on Whitley Links during the 1780s. The beast grew to a staggering height of 5ft 9ins at its shoulders, eventually weighing in at a massive 216 stones.

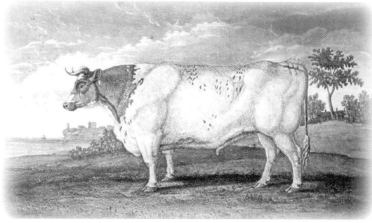

Thomas Bewick's famous engraving of the Whitley Fat Ox.

As a local legend, the Whitley Ox was so big and cumbersome that when it was due for slaughter in March 1789, it created a massive public spectacle – so much so that it took seven days to walk the ten miles to Newcastle slaughter house through sizeable crowds.

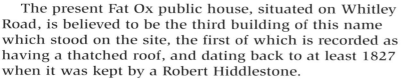

The Ox became a talking point amongst many locals and its subsequent local fame prompted Thomas Bewick to create a copperplate etching (and drawings) of the beast, all of which were published in April 1789.

The present Fat Ox public house, situated on Whitley Road, is believed to be the third building of this name which stood on the site, the first of which is recorded as having a thatched roof, and dating back to at least 1827 when it was kept by a Robert Hiddlestone.

It is implied that this inn was rebuilt in 1869 until it was replaced with the current structure in 1923 as indicated by a stone plaque above the corner door. The letters 'JB' which are also shown on this plaque are indicative of John Buchanan, of the Hanover Square Brewery, who was recorded as landlord from the 1890s through to the 1920s until it was taken over by Ind Coope and Allsop.

THE ROCKCLIFF ARMS

Situated on the south east side of Algernon Place at the corner with Alexandra Terrace, the Rockcliff Arms takes its name from the nearby area on Whitley Bay seafront, generally known and referred to as Rockcliff. Over the years, the spelling of 'Rockcliff' has been corrupted to include the letter 'E' on the end of the word which for some reason has migrated to the current signage of the premises. The original and correct spelling can be seen above the doors of the image below that dates to around 1906.

As nearby Whitley Road developed, construction of the Rockcliff Arms took place prior to 1895, and the basic structure remains largely unaltered. Minor external modifications however have been carried out over the years. In addition to a set of

corner doors, there was also at one time a further set of entrance doors situated in the centre of the pub frontage which led to a very shallow and narrow bar area. A billiards room was also situated to the upper floor.

In more recent years the pub has undergone extensive internal refurbishment which saw the original bar, buffet and snug rooms removed to enlarge the ground floor to an open plan aspect. Despite the alterations, this pub is one of the few establishments still existing in the area which retains the charm and character of a traditional inn.

THE SHIP INN

There have been three Ship Inns at Whitley, the original being a single storey whitewashed stone building, situated on the corner of Front Street (Whitley Road) and Park Avenue (pictured left) and first recorded in 1811 although it is known to have existed some time prior to that date.

In his book, local historian W.W.

Tomlinson described the Ship Inn as '*A quaint old building of one storey*'.

The inn was taken over by the Newcastle Breweries Ltd and completely rebuilt in 1895 to a more traditional design (pictured on the next page and re-named as the 'Ship Hotel'). This building became deservedly popular and served the ever-growing population of Whitley Bay for just over thirty five years before it was decided that a new and larger house was needed to cope with increasing custom. Despite its very short lifespan, the building was demolished in 1930 in order to rebuild the very plain and unappealing curved corner structure which now occupies the same site.

When this new imposing building was built, it was marketed as follows: '*Dominating a corner site with simple modern architecture. Inside it offers splendid accommodation in the shape of a spacious Buffet, a luxurious Buffet-Lounge, Sitting Rooms, ample bar room and a Palm Lounge which is undoubtedly one of the sights of the district. The mural decorations in the Palm Lounge are the work of a well-known North Country artist. It is in this room that the popular musical evenings take place*'.

In the 1970s, the word 'Hotel' was dropped from the name and it simply became the 'Ship', however during the mid-1990s, the traditional character was lost further when it was converted to an Australian themed pub along with a short-lived name change to 'Bar Oz'. Efforts to revive its popularity prompted a further name change to 'Dundees', still retaining the Australian theme but again this was also short-lived before a further name change came, this time as the 'Town House'.

So many pointless name changes serve to confuse people and tend to be disregarded by the local folk who traditionally still (and probably always will) refer to it by the name it has carried for well over 200 years – 'The Ship'.

THE STATION HOTEL

In the summer of 1901, a public meeting was held to protest about proposals to turn the old Post Office buildings which were then situated on the corner of Whitley Road and the Esplanade into a residential hotel. Despite this, building work went ahead in 1904 to create the huge Station Hotel which was to become one of the larger licensed hotels in Whitley Bay.

As a popular hostelry during the holiday season in the heydays of Whitley Bay, it was so named because of its close proximity to Whitley Bay Railway Station. By the

1960s, the building gradually diminished as a hotel and the business continued to run as a public house, with the upstairs floor space being used for occasional entertainment which included singing and dancing. Eventually, the pub also ran into a slow decline before closing down permanently in 2011. Since then, various plans for redevelopment have been submitted, the bulk of which have included proposals to convert the building into self-contained housing apartments.

A fire at the Station Hotel on 7th January 1954 caused extensive damage to the upper floors and roof.

THE VICTORIA HOTEL

Standing prominently on the main street through Whitley Bay, 'The Victoria' or 'The Vic' as it is more popularly known, was at one time the largest and most prevalent building in the village. It began life around 1832 when a John Tinley of North Shields bought an old farm cottage and converted it to become the 'Whitley Park Inn'. When it was sold in 1838, the adjoining cottage was leased to Whitley Colliery and in 1890, was purchased by a James Cowen Landreth, from Berwick who enlarged the building by incorporating two other adjoining cottages. It was possibly his idea to rename the inn as 'The Victoria', probably in honour of the monarch at this time – Queen Victoria.

Landreth retired in 1888 and the inn came into the hands of a Robert Dawson, a publican and mineral water manufacturer.

In 1890, Dawson commissioned further alterations which saw the addition of a third storey to the building along with six bedrooms at a cost of £1000. Soon afterwards, the building was leased to James Anderson & Co., Newcastle Wine & Spirit Merchants.

'The Vic' in 1901.

In 1901, the premises were under the proprietorship of Messrs A.H. Higginbottom & Co. who at that time were a large company advertising as 'Wholesale and Family Wine Merchants, Shippers, Bonders, Blenders, Dealers and Exporters' and a guidebook of this year quaintly describes the pub as follows: *'The most comfortable and best patronised hotel in Whitley is, without question, The Victoria, of which Messrs A.H. Higginbottom and Co. have been for some time the proprietors.*

The position is excellent, occupying as it does the best situation in the village. The house is in every respect commodious and well adapted for the reception of guests. There are large and well-furnished smoking rooms, a spacious dining room, six airy and pleasant bedrooms, and a good billiard room with two tables (Burrough and Watts).

The establishment also provides excellent stabling and coach house accommodation. The cuisine and service are admirable in every respect, and the tariff moderate when the character of the house is considered. A staff of experienced and capable servants is employed, and the welfare of guests scrupulously cared for. Under the able and popular management of the present proprietors the house has gained a widespread reputation and a large connection is enjoyed.

One feature of the establishment is the supply of wines, spirits and malt liquors etc, provided for their customers. The Messrs Higginbottom are extensive dealers in beverages of this kind, and enjoy a high reputation for their excellent quality. They are direct importers, and always have enormous stocks of wines and spirits maturing in their own bonded warehouses.'

In 1930, the central pitched dormer was removed and a new Tudor-style frontage was added, followed by the later construction of four stone ground floor bay windows to become the building it is today.

What was once a fine building, fell victim to the 'theme bar' craze of the 21st century, during which time the pub took a dramatic downturn with bright out-of-character paintwork and signage, and was rather tastelessly renamed as 'The Bedroom'.

Fortunately, the name existed only for a few years and in 2012, the pub underwent refurbishment work and reverted back to its traditional and popular name of 'The Victoria' with more sedate exterior paintwork.

'The Vic' in 1982.

SCHOOLS AND EDUCATION

GORDON COLLEGE AND GORDON SQUARE

In 1884, building work commenced on the large houses known as Gordon Square. A small garden was attached directly to the front of the house, however a larger separate front garden, was situated opposite each house and divided by a narrow access roadway, thereby forming the actual square.

Most of these houses were originally occupied by wealthy professionals and businessmen who would have employed housekeepers. In the mid-1890s, a Miss Eleanor Rimington acquired a large house at No. 1 Gordon Square which stood on the corner of Rockcliffe Street which she opened as a private school. It later became better known as Gordon College.

Gordon College in 1901.

A 1901 guide described the school as follows: '*Gordon College is in a good position, close to the sea. The schoolrooms which are large and airy were specially built for their present purpose. There is a complete staff of English and Foreign resident and visiting mistresses. The system of teaching pursued is thorough, carefully graduated and individual. The time given to evening preparation is strictly limited; if desired, pupils are allowed to return in the evening to school for preparation, where silence is insured and help is given. Special classes are held for painting, physical training (Swedish system) and dancing. Children travelling to and from Shields by train do so morning and evening, in the care of a mistress; by this means, quiet and ladylike behaviour is insured*'.

During the Second World War, the house was requisitioned to house families affected by the blitz and was still occupied in 1947 by homeless families.

In 1979, the property was acquired by a housing association where it became known as 'Gordon House' and managed by Anchor homes as part of a sheltered housing scheme.

Kindergarten classroom inside Gordon College.

Gordon College also had its own Boarding House which was situated at nearby No. 20 Helena Avenue.

WHITLEY NATIONAL SCHOOL

Linked to St Paul's Church, Whitley National School (also known as Church School) was built in 1871 and continued in use up to the early 1920s when it was demolished for redevelopment. The school occupied a site on the corner of Whitley Road (Park View) and Norham Road. The playground area extended into Park View and was replaced by the present 'Hotspur Hall' building with the remainder of the site on Norham Road now being occupied by the present telephone exchange and a small landscaped and seating area.

ROCKCLIFFE SCHOOL

Rockcliffe School (originally known as Whitley South School) was opened on 22nd June 1906 in temporary buildings on Rockcliffe Street, under the headship of Miss Ethel J. Browne and in 1909, it became two separate schools with separate head teachers.

Construction of the present building commenced in 1910 and the school was used for the first time on 1st May 1911 with the official opening date being 10th May 1911. The head teachers were a Mr Turnbull and a Mrs Browne. The schools remained completely separate for fifty one years, until April 1960 when a decreasing child population meant that they were amalgamated to form Whitley Bay South Primary School.

The Infant School was situated on the lower floor and the Junior School upstairs. For many years, the Junior School catered for children up to school leaving age, and children who did not pass a scholarship for the grammar school at the age of eleven remained here for the rest of their school careers.

At the outbreak of the First World War, the school was requisitioned by the Military and closed between October 1914 and September 1919. During this period the school was forced to share buildings with Whitley Bay North Schools (also known as Park School), as a result of which, the children only received a part time education when North School used the building in the morning and South Schools in the afternoon.

The Second World War did not result in a school closure, however it did have a significant impact on school life. Air raid shelters were built in the school yard and were used often during daylight air raids and all children were issued with gas masks. There were many heavy night time air raids which resulted in regular school closures. (If an air raid occurred after midnight, then the school did not open until the afternoon session on the following day.)

Rockcliffe also became a major evacuee centre during Second World War, and there are records of staff manning the school premises until after 10.00 pm to receive evacuees. At one point there were 74 evacuees on the register, many of them being from the London area and some from Holland.

The wartime air raid shelters were demolished in the early 1950s and a nearby garage on Rockcliffe Street was converted to become the School Canteen, and become known as the Rockcliffe Dining Room, remaining in use until July 1971. The site is now occupied by Guardian Court flats.

PARK SCHOOL

In 1907 there were three elementary schools in Whitley Village, the old National School on Whitley Road built in 1871, Whitley South School (Rockcliffe) on Windsor Terrace built in 1906 and Whitley and Monkseaton North School, on Park Avenue built c.1903, otherwise known as Park School.

This school was situated on Park Road between Coquet Avenue and Marine Gardens and originally designed to accommodate 1,020 pupils in three tiers: Boys, Girls and Infants.

Park School later became known as Coquet Park First School and Marine Park First School. The site has since been cleared and the schools have been separated and relocated to the Links and the site of the former Spanish City respectively.

Maypole dancing at Park School in the 1950s.

CHURCHES AND PLACES OF WORSHIP

WHITLEY BAY CONGREGATIONAL CHURCH

The origins of this church date to June 1901 when services were held in a room at the 'Eden Cafe' in Whitley Bay. Almost immediately this room proved too small and services were relocated to larger premises situated within the nearby 'Harrison's Cafe'. A site was later acquired on the corner of Park Avenue and Park Parade and in 1902 a temporary corrugated Iron Hall was erected to serve as a church, school and meeting hall. This was replaced soon afterwards by a brand new building, built in rough-cut red stone, which opened on 28th June 1907 as Whitley Bay Congregational Church.

In 1934 a new church hall and schoolroom was built on the site of the old Iron Hall. These were opened in February 1935 and the building was named 'Livingstone Hall' after the missionary, David Livingstone. The first floor of this building once accommodated the local Labour Exchange. In 1972 the Congregational and Presbyterian Churches merged to create the United Reformed Church. As a result Whitley Bay Congregational Church was renamed Park Avenue United Reformed Church. In 1975 the Church united with St Cuthbert's United Reformed Church to form Trinity United Reformed Church. The old Congregational premises in Park Avenue were sold in 1976 to become Whitley Bay Baptist Church.

Park Avenue and Whitley Bay Congregational Church in 1916.

ST EDWARD'S CHURCH

The first church dedicated to St Edward, was designed by an Edward Kay of Stockton and constructed by a William Gray who also laid out much of nearby Park Parade and Park Avenue. Built on land that was formerly a part of Hickeys Dairy Farm (see page 50) the church was a simple and basic brick building, functional in style, and stood on Roxburgh Terrace close to the corner with Park Avenue and was capable of accommodating a

The original St Edward's Church stood on Roxburgh Terrace. The former St Edward's School adjoins the church. When the new church was built, this building was converted to become the Parish Hall.

congregation of around 250-300 people. It was first opened on 5th March 1911 having an interior oak decor and pitch-pine pews. Soon afterwards, the related St Edwards Catholic School was built on the adjoining land next to the church and opened in January 1914. The school had 5 classrooms and could accommodate up to 250 pupils.

The school closed on 19th July 1968, and the children reconvened at the new replacement Catholic school thereafter – Star of the Sea at West Monkseaton. With an expanding congregation, the need for a replacement church was evident and in 1926, building work commenced on the new St Edward's Church, situated on the corner of Coquet Avenue and Park Road. Designed by Steinlet & Maxwell, it was built by Newcastle contractors, Henry Kelly & Co. at a cost of £15,000 which included the adjoining presbytery. Capable of accommodating a congregation of 500 people, the new church was blessed and opened on 23rd April 1928 by the Bishop of Hexham and Newcastle, Joseph Thorman who led a solemn

The new St Edward's Church. Built in 1926 on the corner of Park Road and Coquet Avenue.

benediction, after which a lunch was held at the Waverley Hotel (later the Rex) on Whitley Bay seafront.

The new church was described as being fashioned in Italian Romanesque style, with an octagonal lantern tower over the four arches of the crossing, and typifying the brick churches of northern Italy. In 1929, the original church on Roxburgh Terrace was converted to become the parish hall.

TRINITY METHODIST CHURCH

Trinity Methodist Church was built in 1889 at a cost of £4,065. The building stood on Whitley Road, on the site of what is now a health centre. On the evening of 29th August 1940, the church was virtually destroyed after a direct hit by a 500lb bomb from enemy aircraft during an air raid attack over Whitley Bay. Two houses in Cheviot View and the nearby bowling green also received direct hits in the same raid. The church, which was damaged beyond repair was later demolished to be replaced in 1955 by a child welfare clinic financed by Northumberland County Council. This image shows the former Church and was taken from the corner of Whitley Road and Algernon Terrace.

ST MARGARET'S CHURCH

The United Methodist Free Church was first built in 1877 and situated at the southern end of Whitley Road at its junction with Margaret Road. At 10.30am on 16th October 1903, a huge fire broke out inside the premises which, within a very short space of time completely destroyed the building. The cause was believed to have been a gas leak, combined with an unknown source of ignition.

The severity of the fire was such that within an hour the premises had been completely burned out with only four walls standing amidst a pile of burning rubble.

Soon afterwards, the building was replaced with a new church which was built on the same site and opened less than two years later on 7th June 1905.

In 1932, it was renamed, St Margaret's Methodist Church with connotations to nearby Margaret Road. The congregation diminished over a period of time and the church closed in 1989, falling into a state of neglect and disrepair. After a further fire in the premises, the church was demolished and replaced by flats which took the name 'Margaret House'.

The original United Methodist Free Church of 1877.

The replacement Church built in 1905 (St Margaret's).

OXFORD STREET METHODIST CHURCH

A short row of houses known as Whitley Cottages (collectively known as Robson's Farm), stood at what is now the site of North Parade and Oxford Street. They were once the residence of local cowman, Thomas Robson. As development of Whitley Village progressed, the land was later purchased by the church authorities following which the cottages were demolished and a small primitive tin chapel erected. On 27th March 1899, the Reverend William Raistrick laid the foundation stone for the new Methodist Church which was designed by a Mr Thomas Edward Davidson of Newcastle. The contractor was Mr Alfred Styan, a prominent local builder. The total construction cost was £3,000 and the church was capable of accommodating 800 people. The opening ceremony was performed on 17th March 1904 by Mrs M.G. Marriott of Monkseaton.

Oxford Street and the Methodist Church.

ST PAUL'S CHURCH

Algernon Percy, 4th Duke of Northumberland provided for a new Church for the parish of Cullercoats which was designated as St Paul's. The correct term for this building was originally 'The church of St Paul, Cullercoats'.

The apparent strangeness of geography being explained by the fact that Cullercoats was a thriving seaport community, when Whitley was little more than a farming village. When St George's church was erected at Cullercoats in 1884, the parish boundaries were re-drawn by the ecclesiastical authority, and St Paul's then became the Parish Church of Whitley and Monkseaton.

Designed by London architect, Anthony Salvin, and built by George Smith & Co. of Pimlico, London, construction work commenced in 1862 in stone in the early English style, consisting of a chancel, nave, aisles, north and south porches with a tower at the south east angle, surmounted by a spire. Eight carved stone faces at the base of the church spire are said to be portraits of people who were prominent locally at the time. The interior was lit by six large paraffin lamps with the first pews being made by Mr Adam Robertson of Alnwick, and the chancel tiled by Minton & Co. of Stoke on Trent.

An ornate lych-gate and stone drinking fountain set into the wall are significant features of the church which was consecrated on 3rd September 1864 by the Bishop of Durham, in whose diocese the village of Whitley then lay, with Algernon, 4th Duke of Northumberland and the Duchess present.

After the ceremony, the duchess was invited to take the first drink from the fountain and remarked that it was 'fine water'. Six bells were afterwards presented to the church by Sir Charles Mark Palmer Bart, MP and in 1866, a clock with chimes was placed into the tower by public subscription.

The first vicar of the church was the Reverend Robert Faulding Wheeler who was also a founder member of the Cullercoats Volunteer Life Brigade.

The churchyard originally covered over one acre of land and completely surrounded the church. The accompanying rectory building which housed the incumbents stood in the grounds to the west of the actual church, however it was vacated and demolished in 1933 when the grounds were reduced in size to accommodate the building of the present shops on Park View that were situated between the church and former church hall on Kings Drive.

The first baptism was that of a Mary Winter which took place on 4th September 1864 and the first marriage was that of Philip Coxon and a Margaret Sedler on 15th October 1864.

It was not until 1870 that the church organ was built and first played by the Reverend J.B. Sykes of Durham who also read the lesson and gave a sermon to celebrate the occasion.

First vicar of St Paul's, the Reverend R.F. Wheeler

The interior of the church was remodelled in 1929 and no burials have occurred there since 1962 as it was intended that the churchyard become a garden of rest. In more recent years, a new addition to the church was made in the form of St Paul's Church Parish Centre. It was designed by Jane Darbyshire, a nationally acclaimed local architect, and constructed in matching fine stone and slate to complement the existing church building. Built on the south side of the church, the L-shaped centre and the original church building enclose a grassy cloister, suitable for outdoor activities.

The church and associated buildings have been Grade II listed since 19th May 1950.

TRANSPORT

WHITLEY TRAMS

In the middle of the 1800s, the section of Whitley Road between Cullercoats to Victoria Terrace was little more than a field with a narrow track running through towards Whitley Village. The road which began at the end of what is now the present Burnside Road, took a slight incline and swept west towards the end of Victoria Terrace where it joined the town centre at the top of South Parade. The road was later straightened and widened to accommodate many of the present shops and buildings.

Alfred Styan, a pioneer builder in Whitley, was largely responsible for construction of many of the buildings towards the western edge of Whitley Road, with terracotta and stone plaques evident above the ground floors.

The Tynemouth and District Electric Traction Company came into being in 1899, and tramlines were laid along Whitley Road as part of a new electrification scheme which saw an extension

A Tynemouth & District Electric Traction Co. Tramcar on Whitley Road, at the corner of Victoria Terrace c.1903.

of the tram service from North Shields and Tynemouth into Whitley Bay via Cullercoats. Regular Services commenced on 10th March 1901, running from the New Quay at North Shields, through Tynemouth and Cullercoats to a terminus which stood opposite the Victoria Hotel at Whitley Bay. Three years later, in 1904, the Victoria terminus was discontinued when a short extension was added to this line which allowed the trams to travel past the Victoria Hotel and continue to a new terminus opposite the Bandstand on Whitley Links via Park Avenue, Park Road and Marine Avenue. By 1931, buses were introduced running the route alternately with tram-cars. The last tram ran on 4th August that year.

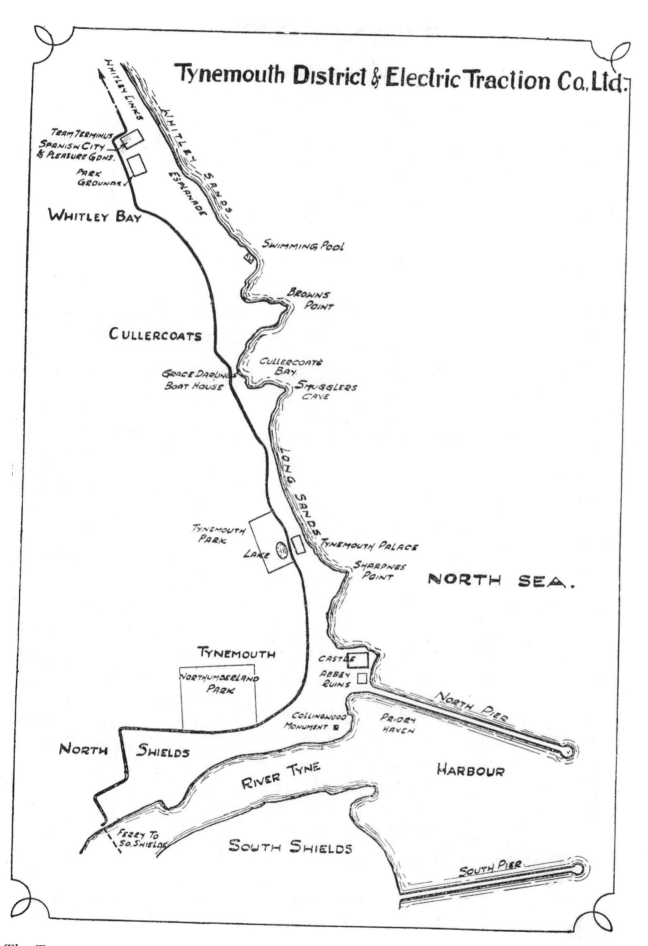

The Tramway route between the New Quay at North Shields and Whitley Bay.

WHITLEY BUSES

Trams had been running in Whitley Bay since 1901, however by 1926, Councillor J.W.B. Thursfield became one of the early pioneers of bus services in Whitley, running a fleet of eight vehicles which he called 'Crescent' and named after the street in which he lived. His first bus ran from the Whitley Terminus which was situated on Front Street, outside the building that was to become Woolworths store and regular services ran to Shiremoor, Backworth, Forest Hall, Killingworth, Newcastle and Morpeth.

Mr Thursfield employed 32 people and his buses were garaged at Horseman's Garage, Marine Avenue with additional garaging space at Shiremoor. He inaugurated the first cheap fares between Whitley and Newcastle, charging 1/- return on quiet days compared to his normal fare of 1/6d or the 1/9d fare on the train.

In 1929, Thursfield sold out to United Automobile Services who later opened the new bus station on Park Avenue in 1935. He then went on to become that company's depot supervisor at Ashington.

Two other local bus operators during this time were Mr J. Howe who ran a service between Blyth and North

An early Tynemouth & District Service bus which alternated with the tram service on the North Shields to Whitley Bay seafront route.

Shields, via Whitley Bay and Monkseaton as well as the County Bus Company who operated from Whitley to Newcastle via New York and Forest Hall. Both of these companies were also taken over by United Automobile Services.

The remaining independent operator was H.W. Hunter of Seaton Delaval, who from 1926 up to 1994, ran a service from Seaton Delaval to North Shields via Whitley Bay and Preston Village.

In these early days, a licence would be granted by the council to anyone who wished to operate a service. In effect, anyone could buy a bus and run it over any route he chose, consequently these early services were often irregular and there was fierce competition between rival concerns and this was particularly evident as the bigger firms began to grow.

Any small operator who refused to sell out stood the risk of being 'run off the road' by his rivals who would either time their buses to run a few minutes before his opponents or even operate services for a week or two without charging fares.

An early Hunter's service bus waits at the Whitley Bay terminus c.1940. The former Council Offices and first Woolworths store are visible in the background.

MISCELLANEOUS

WHITLEY STEAM LAUNDRY

Whitley Bay Steam Laundry, also known as the 'Provincial Laundry', was situated to the rear of Grosvenor Drive, adjacent to the nearby railway line. It started life as a commercial laundry during 1900 before undergoing a number of minor changes over the next 60 years.

An article in the Shields Daily News dated 15th February 1899 stated that: *'The directors of the Provincial Laundry Ltd have decided to build a new steam laundry at the seaside to supply the needs of North Shields, Tynemouth, Whitley and Cullercoats. The laundry will be fitted up with all the most modern appliances, and will be run on the lines of the Low Fell laundry which was recently opened by the same company.'*

This laundry was last mentioned in Kelly's 1962 trade directory.

In 1964-65 the YMCA purchased the building and converted it to create sports and leisure facilities before its official opening date on the 12th November 1965. When the YMCA sold the building it remained unoccupied for a time, and suffered a share of vandalism surviving only as a shell with no remaining evidence of its original internal arrangements. The site was redeveloped in 2012 and is now occupied by a sheltered housing scheme.

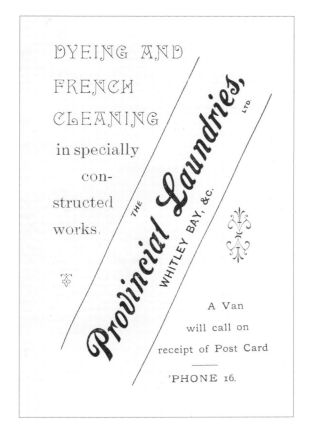

DYEING AND FRENCH CLEANING in specially con-structed works.

The Provincial Laundries, Ltd
WHITLEY BAY, &c.

A Van will call on receipt of Post Card

'PHONE 16.

A view of Whitley Bay Seafront, taken from the Royal Hotel c.1920. The horse-drawn Provincial Laundry Van in the foreground was once a common sight in the town, particularly around the many guest houses and hotels where bedding and linen was collected and delivered after cleaning, almost on a daily basis.

WHITLEY MOTOR COMPANY

Built in the early 1900s, and situated on the corner of Marden Road and Grosvenor Drive, the Whitley Motor Company was better known as St Paul's Garage because of its close proximity to St Paul's Church.

In 1919, following the end of the First World War, the proprietor was a Mr Fred Lund who managed to elicit the services of a Mr Arthur Keen, a vulcaniser who later opened a tyre supply and repair business at the back of Ocean View. Mr Lund lived opposite the garage at No. 2 Grosvenor Drive. During November 1919, Mr Lund and Mr Keen took an exhibitors stand to promote their business at the Motor Show at London Olympia.

As well as carrying out general car and van repair work, the Whitley Motor Company also specialised in car sales along with the supply and maintenance of Triumph motorcycles. The garage also became an official repair centre and agent for the Automobile Association, the Royal Automobile Club and the Auto-Cycle Union.

Up to 1926, the garage was an agent for the Overland Automobile Company based in Indianapolis, USA and in 1921 was commissioned to provide a fleet of 40 of these cars and vans to the Newcastle Electric Supply Company, many of which are seen prior to delivery on the accompanying photograph. The business also included a taxi service which ran from a rank at nearby Whitley Station mainly catering for the benefit of visitors and travellers. Additionally, the garage ran a motor coaching service from the Spanish City entrance with day-trips and outings to various towns and villages in North Northumberland. The business was taken over in 1928 by a Mr John Somerville and despite changing hands a number of times thereafter, it continued life as a garage, a service station and car saleroom until the 1990s after which it functioned as a motor accessory shop and later a general retail unit.

A MYSTERIOUS DEATH

Margaret and Wilhelmina Dewar were elderly sisters who resided together at No. 2 Delaval Road, Whitley Bay. They were both retired school teachers, and a long standing mystery surrounds the demise of Wilhelmina, who was found burned to death in bed at her home. It was around 9pm on Sunday, 22nd March 1908, that Margaret Dewar ran into a neighbour's house shouting that she had just discovered the charred body of her sister, Wilhelmina. Neighbours rushed to the house with Margaret, and found Wilhelmina's body lying on an otherwise unburned bed. There was no evidence of a fire anywhere in the house. When asked about what had happened that day, Margaret said that she had assisted Wilhelmina to bed, and at about 2pm that day she took up some tea, which Wilhelmina refused stating that she wanted to rest. The next time that Margaret checked on her sister was around 9pm that night, when she discovered the gruesome sight. By 10pm, Wilhelmina's body and the scene of her death were being examined by a Dr Campbell who confirmed that she was 'burnt from head to toe', with all her clothes being burned away.

An investigation of the scene confirmed that there were no signs of burning underneath the bedclothes that she was lying on and it was his opinion that she must have been carried into the room, as it was impossible for her to have walked up the stairs – even if she had been assisted. At the inquest, the coroner pressured Margaret Dewar to change her story, as the evidence stated made no sense to him. A Police Officer, Sgt Pinton who had also attended the scene on the night of 22nd March testified that he could not get an intelligible story from Margaret Dewar, as she appeared to be under the influence of drink, however it was not questioned as to whether or not Margaret was actually drunk, or just under extreme emotional distress. Sgt Pinton also testified that he found a part of a burnt wet skirt in the backyard of the house, and one of the neighbours, a Mrs King, testified that she had found some burnt clothing in the downstairs part of the house.

2 Delaval Road, Whitley Bay. The home of Margaret and Wilhelmina Dewar.

On the other hand, the same 1908 source that mentions the burned clothing also covers Dr Campbell's assessment that Wilhelmina Dewar would have to be carried upstairs, for it was impossible for her to have walked there – even with assistance. This may be because both Wilhelmina and Margaret were of an advanced age and Margaret did not have had the physical strength or ability to get Wilhelmina up the stairs. Eventually, Ms Dewar was coerced into stating that Wilhelmina had been burned downstairs, and that she had then been assisted up the stairs by Margaret, only to die in bed later. Once this story was put forward, the case was closed with no attempt to explain where the fire came from or why there was no other evidence of it within the household other than Wilhelmina's remains.

No satisfactory explanation for Wilhelmina's death was ever discovered, and there has been continual speculation that it may have been attributable to a paranormal event, sometimes referred to as SHC (Spontaneous Human Combustion). Spontaneous combustion occurs when an object or a person bursts into flames from a chemical reaction within, apparently without being ignited by an external heat source.

A positive outcome was never established and an open verdict was recorded.

WHITLEY BAY IN THE 70s

Once again, I am greatly indebted to my friend, Chris Wilson for this – the second part of his light hearted overview of 'Whitley Bay in the 70s' where he mainly focuses on the Town Centre. The following edited extracts were taken from his website, where Chris relives more memories of that special era.

So let's jump on board the No. 35 Town Service bus and take another ride through 'Whitley Bay in the 70s' …

INTRODUCTION

'This town ain't big enough for the both of us … and it ain't me who's gonna leave …' This Whitley Bay Town Centre stuff won't perhaps be as exciting as some pages; I mean what did kids get up to in shops? … Buy sweets, Loiter, Get asked to leave. What else was there to do? Here's what – make rude words by rubbing letters off the chalky white writing on Fruit and Veg shop windows (the only one which I recall, so probably the only one, was shortening 'tomatoes' to 'toes' which was naff but we all thought it was hilarious). Pinching fridge boxes from the back yards of electrical shops for sliding down the grassy slopes onto the Prom and having smelly food fights with stuff found in the bins behind the VG shop.

PARK VIEW

(From Marine Avenue traffic lights to St Paul's Church.)

There were many bike and toy shops on this stretch and I spent many an hour in Jack Percy's (very nice man he was), an old-style toy shop with shallow wooden drawers bulging with soldiers, Brittains Farm toys, Dinky catalogues, Airfix kits (and tiny pots of Humbrol enamel), and the most bike-tastic window display in all of Christendom – piles of stickers and Union Jack handlebar flags, parping horns and Pifco lamps, chequered tape, handlebar mirrors, handlegrips … There was nothing better on a Saturday (after *Bagpuss* and *Swap Shop*) than spending pocket money on something for the bike, then rushing back to the shed to fix it on and ride around the streets looking smug. Punctures and worn brake blocks and stuff were always put right by Mr Alsop who had a bike repair shop on the corner opposite. I was in there almost every other week having my rear Chopper tyre replaced after skidding on gravel pretending to be 'The Sweeney'.

Our family were customers of Mr Alsop going right back to my granda who would travel all the way from Marden Estate to have his bike fixed rather than use the much closer Lavericks at Cullercoats. I'm not sure at what point the business closed, after having moved away in early 1981 but the still-recognisable shop later sold musical instruments.

Kind of related to the cycling theme, there was a ladies' boutique called 'Penny Farthing' (what a pity *they* didn't have white chalky writing on their windows for us to rub off). The shop was named after….. get this; an actual 'Penny Farthing' which leant on the wall outside (good job it wasn't a purple Chopper!)

Once, every town worth its salt had a department store (with bits of black gaffer tape holding down the carpet), and Whitley Bay had Ryle's, right on the corner where Park View goes round the bend. I can remember first being there in the late 60s.

Ryle of Whitley Bay

over

half a century of Personal Service

It was considered a rather classy, swanky establishment back then, two floors of leather goods and boxes of tartan hankies which were sold by salmon-faced women doused in Tweed. There were silk headscarves and that sort of thing, as well as silver clothes brushes for sweeping the dandruff from the shoulders of velvet jackets. There was also the posh Hedley Youngs, which I kind of remember boasted an upstairs café with leaded windows and waitresses in black and white uniforms, till it fell from grace to become Thom's and later, Poundstretcher. Of the only other shops I could ever be tooled with were; MacFarlanes just for that lovely rich woollen pong from the rolls of new carpet; DJ Records with its trendier upstairs bit of picture sleeves and coloured vinyl; Tom S. Ford, a china shop on the corner where my Aunty Ella worked and Wilson's Sports (no relation, which I think morphed into Jack Percy's).

WOOLWORTHS

'That's the Wonder of Woolies ...' In a huge loss to the town centre, Woolworth's has now closed for ever. In the 70s at Christmas, I would marvel at their epic, tinselly telly ads. Usually starring Georgie Fame, you got five tinkly and twinkly minutes of 'Yardley', 'Black Magic', and the 'Ronco Buttoneer'. Of course the store's biggest draw was the 'Pick 'n' Mix' at which some kids (not me, coming from a nice family) would stuff the sleeves of their parkas in the pockets, then hide their hands inside and, from between the buttons, pinch sweets from the front of the display. Once in 1974 my mate Jeppa's mum parked her pale green Cortina Mk I outside Woolies and went in to get us some crisps (Tudor Hot Dog 'n' Mustard flavour) and cans of pop to shut us up. So off she went, and quicker than you could say 'Gladstone Adams', we had the windscreen wipers on and were bouncing up and down on the seats, laughing and tooting the horn. Guess who got their legs slapped when she returned.

THE BUS STATION

Off with its head to make space for the current faceless shopping mall. The old Bus Station was not unlike a little microcosmic town in itself; it had a few shops attached – Carricks/Crawfords the bakers, Young Blades where my sister Julie worked and got me free T-shirts with transfers on, a travel shop, a tobacconists and its own nightclub – 'The Sands'.

I was too young to be allowed in there so that's all it gets. Looks like I was missing out on quite a scene, judging by this groovy advert (with those guys giving it loads), and topping it all off was the smokiest poohole of a bus waiting room, always full on

rainy days, the windows steamed up, dripping wet folks with shopping bags, either chain smoking or stuffing down Crawford's Meat Squares and Cheese 'n' Onion crisps.

Any gentlemen needing a quick widdle before the red United bus for West Monkseaton pulled in had to access the cloakroom by crossing the furious 'feathers-flying, pigeon-squish' of buses tearing round the station. Then, having made it safely inside, you were smacked in the gob by the weapons-grade odour of Life-Guard disinfectant and a 2p charge for the sort of trap in which you might catch Peter Wyngarde standing with a lorry driver. There were only two or three dangling damp sheets of slidey Izal (an industrial 'anal cleansing film', usually found in the toilets of factories and other places where you were not encouraged to sit all day reading the 'Chronicle'). These were usually left over to make yourself presentable, as eager draws on cigarettes, phlegm-rattling coughs, trouser-trumpets and various other unexplained sounds from the adjoining cubicles that were heard only hitherto in Victorian hospitals, echoed around the ochre coloured porcelain.

THE POST OFFICE

A lovely old building with a wood-panelled interior which was pulled down with the Bus Station. There was always a bustling rush in the goods yard around the back, with the red Morris Minor 'Post Office' and the yellow 'Post Office Telephones' vans. Morris Minors were surely insisted upon *en-masse* by a person of good humour because of that distinctive 'farty' noise they made when changing gear.

Well this takes me back – vans in those days almost had cheeky little '*Tootles the Taxi*' faces. There was also a related yard at the bottom of Norham Road (the Telephone Exchange, with the heavy wooden gates) where the yellow PO vans would slip into their pyjamas and go to sleep.

WHITLEY ROAD
(From St Paul's Church to ... who gives a monkey's!)

'*It's all at the Co-op ... NOW!*' ... Well not as we knew it because it moved from its attractive corner site opposite the church to where Lipton's store was (opposite the no-longer-there-Bus Station). Co-ops were always in nice 'Quakery' buildings.

There was another Lipton's further along Whitley Road with a very busy sausage-beans-and-chips type of restaurant upstairs, but now it's a health-supplement store for those men who walk around scowling with imaginary rolls of carpet under their arms. There was nowt worse than having a mam and three older sisters and being forced to go along when they were shopping for clothes. I'll not stir up any more childhood bitterness towards girls' fashions of the time, so for Topaz and Books' Fashions you can add your own memories. I'm off ... (although there was a lady who worked in Topaz who I used to fancy called Rosemary, but I was only 4 years old, so a fat chance there.)

T&G Allan not only had a classic toy department on the first floor (near the spiral staircase) where we bought catapults and jokey things like horns with a suction pad to stick on your forehead and snappy gum, but also a very hip 'in-the-groove' record department in the basement. T&G Allan would have gotten a monster plug here for never having lost its charm, warm staff, and comfort zone-ness right up to the present. But tragically for our town, after over 150 years of wonderment, T&G Allan has ceased trading.

All I can remember about the rest of Whitley Road was a surfing/diving shop where we bought skateboard things (opposite the clinic) and a brill model shop further down (and I'm sure that same shop used to sell terrapins).

OTHER FLOTSAM and JETSAM

My granda told me way back then of a bloke who lived in Embleton or somewhere far up the Coast who would actually cycle down to Whitley Bay just to get his fish and chips from the Arcade (the world's bestest chippy)!

We would often gather up the discarded empty pop bottles from the late-summer-afternoon Links and with the return money from the shop opposite the Berkeley Tavern we'd each have enough to buy hamburger and chips and a can of dandelion and burdock from Torres next door (quite a selection of chippies back then).

I had a bit of a childhood obsession with cars, and some of us would cycle round the garages collecting brochures for an imaginary school project (otherwise you were told to go away). Just look at some of these great names: there was Colebrook & Burgess (VW, Audi, NSU, Volvo) at Hillheads, where Morrisons is now; Wingrove (Citroen) which became a carpet shop; Minories (Hillman, Humber, Simca) at Preston Grange; Taylors (Vauxhall, Bedford) opposite the Spanish City and at West Monkseaton; R.

Wilson (Austin, Morris, Wolseley, MG) on Cauldwell Lane, Monkseaton; Foxhunters Garage (Triumph, Rover, Land Rover); Oxford Street Garage (Skoda); Davidsons (Ford) at the bottom of Whitley Road; a Datsun garage (another Minories I think) at Whitley Lodge; and Renault at Shiremoor (can't remember the name – Brown's or something).

As part of the car fixation I suppose, I could also often be seen skulking shiftily about on Saturdays in the Chris Dawson shop (later became a tanning studio) on Station Road, fancying that I looked like a potential Roger Clarke in my 'rally jacket' with a Castrol GTX patch sewn on. Opposite Dawson's was Rickards, the estate agent where my mam worked as a secretary for a few years in the mid-70s. Prior to this, she worked for a company called Burton Coin Machines (owned by the pervasive Harry Swaddle, the man at the helm of many other Whitley Bay 'thrill-quadrants' including the Coliseum). This was essentially a small team of repair men with 'walkie-talkies' who drove around the amusement arcades fixing the machines. During school holidays I would sometimes go along for the ride, or just hang around in their workshop playing pinball all day, with 'Seasons in the Sun' playing on the radio.

Now this is where it starts to get boring (if it hasn't already) because that's all I can be bothered to recall. There are a lot of stores and businesses that still remain from three decades ago, but give *that* lot a mention and it starts amounting to free advertising – and we need the money first!

CHURCHILL PLAYING FIELDS

This was the biggest and bestest with several acres of sports fields and pitches for healthy folk (usually PE teacher dads who garnered neat little rows of prize banners on the rear windows of their Hillman Hunter estate cars). The proper fun part was the kids' play area, smack-dab in the middle, and fenced-off to discourage the dog owners of Holywell Avenue from exercising giant poodles. A well-thought-out landscaped playground was provided with a central hill through which concrete tunnels ran, somewhere to scurry through on your honkers, bang your head, or indulge in a secret piddle. There were the usual swings and things, one of those treacherous rocking horses with 4 or 5 seat pads (great if you

stood on the foot rests, held on to the handles and 'got it going' – responsible for chopping off a few hands I'll bet), a couple of climbing frames shaped like giant spiders, one big enough to walk or ride your bike under. Now Churchill was extra special for younger kids. I remember my sisters taking me to the play area where in summer you could hire a trike or small bike for a few pence from the council man in a tiny little wooden shed (a nicer cousin of the lighthouse car park attendant). The shed remained there for years, and bikes inside, locked-up at night with only a small padlock - nothing was pinched or damaged until around the late 70s when it all went up in smoke. Soon the tunnels became teenage drinking dens (nowt to do with me) so that was the end of any early childhood memories there. The large running track was often used in summer for, well, running tournaments which were a bit drab, until 1978 when The Hell Drivers came from the USA (it said on the posters). Those guys would perform stunts such as drive up ramps and onto two wheels, pop wheelies, jump over lines of old bangers, and ride motorbikes through flaming hoops. That was more like it, and from then on any kid with a bike and a plank of wood would attempt similar things. Luckily hospitals were much nicer places to put Humpty together again in those days (there is still a scar on my forehead from going over the handlebars).

WHITLEY PARK (or the LIBRARY PARK)

This used to be a well-tended public garden with a little stream trickling through on a concrete channel, with pathways and a couple of humpback bridges, until it reached a stone waterfall feature which never seemed to work (there was a natural spring in the park, which may have been the source). This was not just somewhere to disappear into following any incidents in the Spanish City, but a place full of deep bushes and dens and trees to climb. The park was a busy maze of interconnecting walks, flower beds and grassy areas, always full of life. I suppose the only decidedly 'wicked' thing we ever got up to here was to dare each other to go into the disabled part of the public toilets, pull the alarm cord and then 'leg' it.

CRAWFORD PARK

Crawford Park is just round the corner from our old house in Paignton Avenue, West Monkseaton, and was the centre of existence until we moved down to Brighton Grove in 1974. The tennis courts, bushes and bowling greens (lovely, summery-sounding and satisfying 'clonk' when the bowls knocked together) are almost as we left them. The bowling pavilion sold 'sports mixtures' in little paper bags and glass bottles of heavenly pop in then-odd flavours like blackcurrant and, er, some red one. We had dens all around the perimeter bushes, moving on to the next following objections from the miserable lot  (usually arms-folded women with those 'Paul and Linda' haircuts) whose gardens backed on. The main den was just behind the pavilion with a gap into which you rode your bike like the Batcave. An older kid I knew from school (Paul something, but can't recall his second name) and me would hide in the bushes waiting for Sid the park keeper to wander past to a serenade of 'Sid-ney, Sid-ney, you're not fit to wipe my bum ...' At the bottom entrance to the park lived a guy who had something to do with – or maybe he was the Mayor – who couldn't seem to grasp the concept of kids and fun and nor did his big black doberman.

OTHER PARKS

These were of less interest, but the one over the railway footbridge near the site of the old Monkseaton Station goods yard had two fabulous climbing frames, one shaped like a space rocket and one a huge space capsule. There were many play areas in and around the Hillheads estate, best of which was up near the Foxhunters roundabout boasting a giant 'banana' slide with a box at the top you could sit in, and a giant spinning 'witches hat' (another thing banned through loss of limbs). And Souter Park, well, nothing to us but a treetop den accessed by climbing on top of the bogs and the nearby ovular grassy miniature bike 'race track' – still there I think.

THE CINDER TRACK & HOLYWELL DENE

The Cinder Track is the disused railway which begins in the bushes to the left of the entrance to Hartley Avenue, down through the subway beneath Monkseaton Drive, past the odd pile of free newspapers dumped in a ditch, and on for literally yonks to The Avenue at Seaton Delaval and New Hartley. Whether during the school holidays or at the weekend, we would get the bikes out, pump up the tyres, make sure all nuts were tight (with special Chopper spanner), and spend all day in the open countryside beyond where Whitley Lodge and the golf course go back to nature.

'*Freedom is a dusty road, heading to a highway ...*' My favourite stretch was on reaching the bridge for the Beehive Road (or Hartley Lane), ringed by endless cornfields as tyres sloshed through crispy-topped cowpats, before dipping down into the dark woodland of Holywell Dene, whispering trees and the ghostly silhouette of the footbridge. Up onto the bridge (it must have been brill standing on here when steam trains chuffed through the trees and passed beneath) and riding like Billy-O along the long, twisty path, past the top farm and down to the old mill (though now a ruin, unless it has gone completely). Around 1975/6 there were a couple of old rusty cars parked outside and dusty net curtains up at the windows suggesting someone may have still lived there, which was creepy in itself. Over the stone bridge crossing the dene, and a very steep climb up to the white Delaval Arms on top of the hill (we weren't allowed a couple of cold refreshing pints in those days) and back across scenic clifftops, past the island, along the Prom, and home. For other places to explore there were plenty public footpaths and bridleways, or just wherever we fancied. Along the Cinder Track past Holywell Dene and obscured by a copse of trees beside a small lake was a bird-watching hide made of telegraph poles with 'Fort Jackson' scratched into the concrete base. From other tracks leading to where Holywell Dene snakes round to meet Seaton Sluice you could reach two Delaval follies, the Obelisk and Starlight Castle. Clin and I were once approached by a herd of cows (bit like South Parade) near here so, what to do, we both stood up on a convenient farm gate and widdled on them, which must have tickled them no end.

MARDEN QUARRY

Certain Public Information films notwithstanding, I'm afraid to say the allure of the Quarry was indeed heightened in that maybe, just maybe, something exciting might happen or someone might fall in, beset by creatures of the deep. But boys will be boys. I remember an occasion when Clin, Wardy and myself walked precariously out across the frozen mini-lake as the ice began to crackle beneath — amazingly the ice held the three of us till we slid our way slowly to the edge, but that was enough

of that. All year round there were always a few ropes, with maybe a car tyre attached, tied to the tall trees which swung out over the fridge-infested water. Indeed, the quarry could take pride in its own abandoned Ford Anglia and a Presto trolley or two.

THE PLAYHOUSE

My first memory of this place was being forced to watch 'Thoroughly Modern Millie' with my sisters in 1968, but fortunately I was sick halfway through after copious little tubs of vanilla ice cream (with the blue plastic spoons) so off home we went. Like all kids through the ages (except that miserable lot nowadays) we would go to watch the

usual Saturday morning Cinema Club – cartoons, B-movies, scary information films, and a sort of talent thing where kids would climb on stage and sing or do naff impersonations (usually annoying 5-year-old kids in berets, going 'Mmm Betty ...'). Wardy, Clin and me later managed to wheedle our way in to help out with the theatre backstage, and one of the crazy things we had to do was to climb a long way up a ladder to the upper fly's area, to operate the big handle-wheel which lowered or raised the curtain. It would have been a hoot had one of us slipped and tumbled the 40 feet to our doom. Fun though, and sometimes we helped out painting the scenery too (and as if that weren't enough, we got to meet Ronnie Carroll). Of course we went and abused it all, as one of our other friends, Daimler, worked as an usherette and would open the fire doors on Marine Avenue so we could saunter in to watch films without paying ... Tsk Tsk ... !

THE LIBRARY

Wasn't there always something 'big' about picking up your recently-applied-for Library Card from the lady with specs at the info desk. Many rainy or cold Saturday afternoons were spent in here reading 'Autocar' and 'Motor' (and, naturally to giggling pre-pubescent kids, Page 3 of 'The Sun'). Built the same year I was born, I wish they had just restored this place, or maybe modernised it a bit, instead of hiring the bulldozer. Even if whoever that weird person it is continues to leave his/her dried bogeys and athletes' foot powder squashed between the pages of the books.

THE ICE RINK

On rainy Saturdays in the spring of 78, we'd catch the 308 bus up to the Ice Rink, the stage for many a bruised, icy bum, and spend the first half hour of the morning session in a pair of ill-fitting hired skates. (I always pitied the man with the stinky fingers from handling all those poor people's trainers.)

We used to hold onto the sides till balance was restored, attempts at speed-skating, and skidding to an abrupt stop to spray unsuspecting girls with ice and 'Mr Blue Sky or 'Baker Street' (hate that song) on repeat play.

PARKERS ICE LOLLIES

At the top of Eastbourne Gardens were two tiny grocery shops, Florrie's and Parker's. The latter was run by a very nice man, John, with his wife and brother Ken (that's two different people by the way) and they sold the top-notchest home-made penny ice lollies with the tastiest, squinkiest flavours ever, like dandelion & burdock and cream soda (all made with a surely disproportionate amount of Sodastream concentrate), but hey – who honestly gave a monkey's about their teeth when sweets and pop were on the agenda.

THE SCHOOL BUS

We used to wait for the school bus to Star of The Sea, from the top of Eastbourne Gardens right next to Scotts bakery – a gorgeous smell in those days when they baked their bread round the back! But each Monday morning inside the bus, the air would be afresh with cleanliness, Vosene and Lenor. This would gradually wear off through the week, and by Friday it was back to that familiar unwashed pungence of stale Digestive biscuits and tallow. (And why did girls sitting on the back seats have to insist on cheese and onion crisps.)

KALA + WBAB

We all remember those beastly Whitley Bay Aggro Boys, that's if they actually did exist in any form other than someone's badly-scrawled graffiti. But the question on everyone's lips was: just who or what were KALA? Was it just some skinhead who fancied himself as 'a bit of a lad'? My beer tokens are firmly wagered on 'Killingworth and Longbenton Aggro'.

WHITLEY BAY STREET CRUISERS

American Graffiti had Richard Dreyfuss and Harrison Ford. Whitley Bay had this cap-sleeved hairy bunch who burbled, tootled and throbbed their way around the one-way on weekend nights in their 'jacked-up' Cortinas. Furry dice, furry dashboards, furry sideburns, 'Kev' and 'Donna' on the green windscreen strip, obligatory (and illegal) orange lights beneath the sills to light up the road, and the odd red Viva with Starsky and Hutch stripes and Wolfrace wheels. Yes these fashion sharks were serious, even once risking their chrome chain-link steering wheels on an outing all the way to Land's End as we see on the photo, and, yes, that's my brother-in-law Paul on the right, with the go-faster blond streaks and bony ankles.

THE RALEIGH CHOPPER

The faithful Wilson Chopper, dayglow boyhood companion and getaway vehicle to many a shenanigan, so special was he that after 30-odd years I can still recall his serial number: NB4046066. Amazingly stolen thrice, and each time recovered by the lads on Laburnum Avenue, the most memorable time was in the Spring of 1975. I was riding on the Links when a much older kid asked *'Giz a shot'* and promptly done off with the bike of course, so after me bubbling not unreasonably like a 9-year-old all the way home, the police came, made notes, then drove me around the Spanish City and along the coast and there, at Cullercoats, was the desperado pedalling along the sea front. I can still see his terrified face as he was well and truly nabbed. I arrived home sadly one Saturday night in 1977 to find my brother Gary – in an uncalled-for move that would delight a modern day NT Council – administering a liberal coating of black Hammerite to my bike-ular chum. Harumphhh … No-one, but no-one should ever mess with a man's wheels.

The 70s for me started to lose its 'true 70s-ness' after 1978. I will always be a fierce advocate of the years from 1970 to 1977, maybe something to do with being at the wonderful Star of the Sea school and certain friends and the astonishingly fab music of those times. Perhaps things started to become more serious when there was gradually less Euro-pop glitz and more New Wave attitude, or just through growing up and having to move on to a deeply unpleasant high school. Now an adult you can safely say I still have quite a few childhood horses to round up, otherwise these pages would not have happened, but there's still a lot of work to do and memories to add before we're done …